Basics of ...
Beekeeping

Basics of ...
Beekeeping

An Introductory Course For Everyday People

THE HISTORY OF BEES, DIRECTIONS FOR
OBTAINING THE GREATEST AMOUNT OF PURE
HONEY WITH THE LEAST POSSIBLE EXPENSE –
MANAGING AN APIARY.

*LORENZO LORRAINE LANGSTROTH,
M. QUINBY, AND OTHER CONTRIBUTORS*

Basics of ...

is an imprint of

ABSOLUTELY AMAZING eBOOKS

Published by Whiz Bang LLC, 926 Truman Avenue, Key West, Florida 33040, USA.

Basics of ... Beekeeping copyright © 2014 by Gee Whiz Entertainment LLC. Electronic compilation/ paperback edition copyright © 2014 by Whiz Bang LLC. *A Bee Keeper's Manual* and *Mysteries Of Bee-Keeping Explained* were originally published in 1853.

All rights reserved. No part of this book may be reproduced, scanned, or transmitted in any form or by any means, electronic or mechanical, including photocopying, recording, or any information storage and retrieval system, without permission in writing from the publisher. Please do not participate in or encourage piracy of copyrighted materials in violation of the authors' rights. Purchase only authorized ebook editions.

While the authors have made every effort to provide accurate information, neither the publisher nor the authors assume any responsibility for errors, or for changes that occur after publication. Further, the publisher does not have any control over and does not assume any responsibility for author or third-party websites or their contents. Statement by Archivist: *Much of the material in this book is in the public domain because it was published in the United States before 1923.*

For information contact:
Publisher@AbsolutelyAmazingEbooks.com

ISBN-13: 978-0692240670
ISBN-10: 0692240675

So work the Honeybees.
Creatures that by a rule in Nature, teach
The art of order to a peopled kingdom.

- William Shakespeare

CONTENTS

CHAPTER ONE
ABOUT HONEYBEES

CHAPTER TWO
A BRIEF HISTORY OF BEEKEEPING

CHAPTER THREE
APICULTURE

CHAPTER FOUR
HONEY AND POLLEN

CHAPTER FIVE
THE HIVE

CHAPTER SIX
THE APIARY

CHAPTER SEVEN
IRRITABILITY OF BEES

CHAPTER EIGHT
BREEDING

CHAPTER NINE
BEE PASTURAGE

CHAPTER TEN
BEESWAX

CHAPTER ELEVEN
PROPOLIS

CHAPTER TWELVE
FEEDING

CHAPTER THIRTEEN
PUTTING ON AND TAKING OFF BOXES

CHAPTER FOURTEEN
SWARMING

CHAPTER FIFTEEN
ARTIFICIAL SWARMS

CHAPTER SIXTEEN
SWARMS THAT LOSE THEIR QUEEN

CHAPTER SEVENTEEN
PRUNING

CHAPTER EIGHTEEN
AVOIDING DISEASED STOCK

CHAPTER NINETEEN
ENEMIES OF BEES

CHAPTER TWENTY
PROTECTING HONEY FROM THE MOTH

CHAPTER TWENTY-ONE
ROBBERIES

CHAPTER TWENTY-TWO
MELTING DOWN OF COMBS

CHAPTER TWENTY-FOUR
WINTERING BEES

CHAPTER TWENTY-FIVE
THE BEHAVIOR OF BEES

CHAPTER TWENTY-SIX
STRAINING HONEY AND WAX

CHAPTER TWENTY-EIGHT
COLONY COLLAPSE DISORDER AND GMO'S

CHAPTER TWENTY-NINE
PURCHASING STOCKS AND TRANSPORTING BEES

Bee gathering pollen.

PREFACE

It is folly to expect success in beekeeping without proper knowledge of the nature and instincts of bees. And most treatises neglect the several chapters of information necessary for a beginner.

This work contains much original matter not found elsewhere. These additions are the results of my own experience. The chapter on "Loss of Queens" alone will save anyone enough in one season to be worth many times more than the cost of this book. The same might be said of those chapters on diseased brood, artificial swarms, wintering bees, and similar topics.

If such a work could have been placed in my hands twenty years ago, I would have been saved hundreds of dollars by the information.

- Moses Quinby

INTRODUCTION
TWO PRINCIPLES OF BEEKEEPING

Many persons have been unable to control their astonishment on seeing me open hive after hive in my apiary, removing the combs covered with bees and shaking them off in front of the hives; exhibiting the Queen, transferring the bees to another hive, and dealing with them as if they were as harmless as so many flies.

In the early ages of the world, honey was almost the only natural sweetener; and the promise of "a land flowing with milk and honey" had a significance, the full force of which is difficult for us to realize. The honeybee not only has the ability to store up delicious honey for its own use, but also displays certain properties which suit it to be domesticated.

One of the peculiarities that allows man to domesticate so irascible an insect has never, to my knowledge, been clearly stated as a great and controlling principle.

It may be expressed thus:

1. *A honeybee never volunteers an attack, or acts on the offensive, when it is gorged with honey.*

The man who first attempted to lodge a swarm of bees in an artificial hive was doubtless agreeably surprised at the ease with which he was able to accomplish it. For when the bees are intending to swarm, they fill their honey-bags to the utmost capacity. This is so they have supplies for commencing operations immediately in their new habitation; and so they won't starve if several stormy days should follow their emigration.

Bees issue from their hives in a most peaceable mood; and unless they are abused, will allow themselves to be treated with great familiarity. The hiving of bees by those who understand their nature can almost always be accomplished without the risk of any annoyance.

True, a few improvident or unfortunate bees occasionally come forth without the soothing supply of honey; and are filled with gall for anyone who dares meddle with them. Such radicals are always to be dreaded, for they must vent their anger on something, even though they lose their life in the act.

A second peculiarity in the nature of the bee may be thus stated:

2. *Bees cannot, under any circumstances, resist the temptation to fill themselves with liquid sweets.*

If we can call their attention to a treat of running sweets when we wish to perform any operation that might provoke them, we may be sure they will accept it, and under its genial influence allow us to do what we please without fear of molestation.

We must always be careful not to handle them roughly for they never allow themselves to be pinched or hurt without thrusting out their stinger. I always keep a small watering pot or sprinkler in my apiary, and as soon as the cover of a hive is taken off, and the bees exposed, I sprinkle them gently with water sweetened with sugar. They help themselves with the greatest eagerness and in a few moments are in a perfectly manageable state.

The truth is, bees managed on this plan are always glad to see visitors, and you cannot look in upon them too often, for they expect at every call to receive a sugared treat by way of a peace offering.

I can oversee a large number of hives, performing every operation that is necessary for pleasure or profit, without running the risk of being stung. Those who are timid may, at first, use a protective bee suit; though they will soon discard everything of the kind, unless they are among those to whom the bees have a special aversion. Such unfortunates are sure to be stung whenever they show themselves in the vicinity of a beehive, and they will do well to give beekeeping a very wide berth.

Apiarians have for many years employed the smoke of tobacco for subduing their bees. It deprives them, at once, of all disposition to sting, but it ought never to be used for such a purpose. If the construction of the hives will not permit the bees to be sprinkled with sugar water, the smoke of burning paper or rags will answer every purpose, and the bees will not resent it; whereas when they recover from the effect of the tobacco, they frequently remember, and not in a kind way, the person who administered the nauseous dose.

Let all your motions about your hives be gentle and slow. Accustom your bees to your presence; never crush or injure them in any operation; acquaint yourself fully with the principles of management detailed in this treatise, and you will find that you have no more reason to dread the sting of a bee than fear the horns of your favorite cow, or the heels of your faithful horse.

- L.L. Langstroth

The Queen and her court.

CHAPTER ONE
ABOUT HONEYBEES

How doth the little busy bee
Improve each shining hour,
And gather honey all the day
From every shining flower!
-Isaac Watts

The honeybee is a winged insect that collects nectar and pollen, produces wax and honey, and lives in large communities. Bees were domesticated for their honey around the Neolithic period. They are usually kept in hives.

Honey is produced by bees as a food source. In order to produce a single jar of honey, foraging honeybees must travel the equivalent of three times around the world.

Bees can flourish only in large numbers as a colony. In a solitary state, a single bee is almost as helpless as a newborn child. It is unable to endure even the ordinary chill of a cool summer night.

HONEYBEE CLASSIFICATION

Honeybees belong to the superfamily *Apoidea*, the order *Hymenoptera*, the family *Apidae*, and the genus *Apis*. The most familiar bee is the *Apis mellifera*.

Bees are found on every continent except Antarctica.

Basics of ... Beekeeping

THREE KINDS OF BEES

If you examine a colony of bees, you will find three different kinds of bees in the hive.

1. A bee of peculiar shape, commonly called the *Queen Bee*.

2. Some hundred, more or less, large bees called *Drones*.

3. Many thousands of a smaller kind called *Workers*, or common bees (like those seen on blossoms).

A vast amount of cells in a hive are filled with honey and beebread; but a number of other cells contain eggs and immature Workers and Drones. A few cells of unusual size are devoted to rearing young Queens.

QUEEN

WORKER

DRONE

DESCRIPTION OF QUEEN

The Queen is the mother of the entire family; her duty is only to deposit eggs in the cells. During the height of the breeding season she will often lay from two to three thousand eggs a day!

Her abdomen has its full size very abruptly where it joins the trunk or body, and then gradually tapers to a point. She is longer than either the Drones or Workers, but her size, in other respects, is a medium between the two. In shape she resembles the Worker more than the Drone; and, like the Worker, has a sting, but will not use it for anything below royalty. She is nearly destitute of down, or hairs; a very little may be seen about her head and trunk. This gives her a dark, shining appearance, on the upper side – some are nearly black. Her legs are somewhat longer than those of a Worker; the two posterior ones, and the under surface, are often a bright copper color. In some a yellow stripe nearly encircles the abdomen at the joints and meets on the back. Her wings are about the same as a Worker's, but as her abdomen is much longer, they only reach about two-thirds the length of it.

For the first few days after leaving the cell her size is less than after she has assumed her maternal duties. She seldom, perhaps never, leaves the hive, except when leading a swarm, or to meet the Drones in the air for the purpose of fecundation.

DESCRIPTION OF WORKERS
Workers are females whose "egg-bags" are so imperfectly developed that they are incapable of breeding. However, they retain the female instinct of providing devoted attention to feeding and rearing the brood.

That's not all. The defense of the colony against enemies, the construction of the cells, the storing of honey and beebread, the rearing of the young – in short, the whole work of the hive, the laying of eggs excepted – is carried out by these industrious little Workers.

As all labor rests on these Worker bees, they are provided with a sack, or bag, for collecting nectar and pollen. On their legs are basket-like cavities where they pack the pollen of flowers into little pellets, convenient to bring home. They range the fields collecting pollen, secrete wax, construct combs, prepare food, nurse the young, bring water for the use of the community, obtain propolis to seal up all crevices about the hive, stand guard, and keep out intruders, etc.

Well armed, these fearless Workers are equipped with a stinger that contains a virulent poison – however they will not use it unless molested. If attacked they generally defend themselves only sufficient to allow an escape.

The number of Workers in a hive varies. A good swarm ought to contain 15,000 or 20,000. And in large hives, strong colonies that are not reduced by swarming, they frequently number two or three times that many during the height of the breeding season.

DESCRIPTION OF DRONES

Drones are stingless male bees whose main purpose is to be available for breeding.

They begin to make their appearance in April or May, according to the climate and the strength of the stock. They require about twenty-four days for their full development from the egg.

When the family is large and honey abundant, a brood of Drones is reared; the number depends on the yield of honey and size of the swarm more than anything else. As honey becomes scarce, they are subsequently destroyed.

Drones are nearly twice the size of a Worker bee. Their bodies are large and rather clumsy, covered with short hairs or bristles.

Their abdomen terminates very abruptly, without the symmetry of the Queen or Worker. Their buzzing, when on the wing, is louder, and altogether different from the others. They seem to be of the least value of any in the hive. They do not work, do not forage for pollen or nectar. On occasion they assist by keeping up the animal heat that's necessary to maintain in an old hive after a swarm has left.

Maybe one Drone in a thousand is called upon to perform the duty for which he was designed – mating with new Queens and fertilizing them on their mating flights.

As a general rule, in colonies too weak to swarm, no Drones are produced: they are not needed, for in such hives, with no young Queens being raised, they would be only useless consumers of the colony's resources.

WHERE TO GET YOUR BEES?

Honeybees can be introduced into your hive by capturing a swarm, purchasing a nuc (short for nucleus) or buying a package of bees. The most widely used method is package bees.

Package bees can be ordered through local beekeeping associations or beekeeping supply companies.

A package usually contains 3 pounds of bees, consisting of several thousand workers and one queen suspended in a cage from the top of the package. The queen is kept separate from the workers as she most likely originated from a different hive. This separation in transit allows the workers and queen to get used to each other's chemical scent.

You will find more information about sources and current pricing of bees elsewhere in this book. Acquiring your hive of bees is as simple as ordering a book from Amazon. And you can be confident that your bees will arrive healthy and disease free. Modern commerce at your service.

ANATOMY OF A HONEYBEE

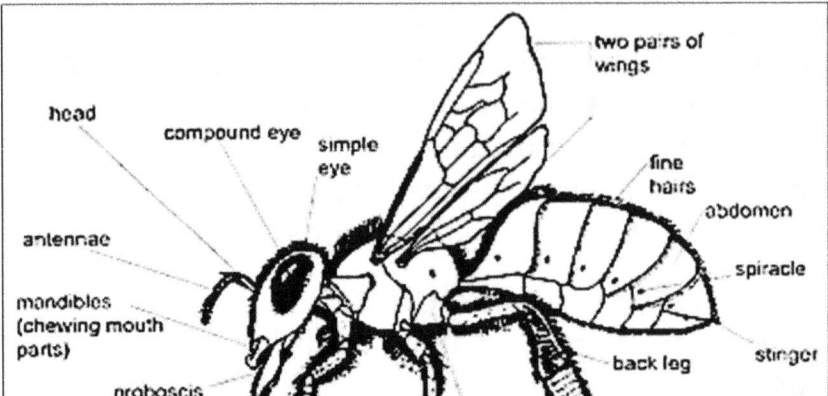

LONGEVITY OF BEES

The Queen will live four, and sometimes, though very rarely, five years.

With the exception of the Queen, none of the bees live to be a year old.

Because the life of a Drone is usually cut short by violence, it is not easy to ascertain its precise age limit, but it is estimated at about four months.

The Workers live six or seven months. However, their longevity very much depends upon exposure to injurious influences and severe labors. Those reared in the spring

Lorenzo Lorraine Langstroth

and early summer, on whom the heaviest labors of the hive necessarily devolve, do not live for more than two or three months, while those Workers bred at the close of summer and in early autumn, being able to spend a large part of their time in repose, attain a much greater age.

Notched and ragged wings, instead of gray hairs and wrinkled faces, are the signs of old age in the bee. They appear to die rather suddenly, and often spend their last days, and sometimes even their last hours, in useful labors.

The age that individual members of the community attain must not be confounded with that of the colony itself. With bees continually replacing themselves, communities of bees have been known to occupy the same domicile for a great number of years. I have seen flourishing colonies that were twenty years old, and some more than forty years old! Such cases have led to the erroneous opinion that bees are a long-lived species.

MOST BROOD IN SPRING

In spring and first of summer, when nearly all the combs are empty, and food abundant, they rear broods more extensively than at any other period (towards fall more combs are filled with honey, creating less room for a brood). During these periods, the hive becomes crowded with bees, and royal cells are constructed to allow the Queen to deposit her eggs.

When some of these young Queens are advanced sufficiently to be sealed over, the old Queen along with the greater part of her subjects leave the hive for a new location (called *swarming.*)

These swarmers collect in a cluster and if put into an

empty hive commence their labors anew: constructing combs, rearing brood, and storing honey, only to be abandoned the succeeding year for yet another tenement.

In July or August, soon after the swarming season is over, the bees expel the Drones from the hive. They sometimes sting them, and sometimes gnaw the roots of their wings, so that when driven from the hive, they cannot return. If not treated in either of these summary ways, the Drones are so persecuted and starved that they soon perish.

REARING THE QUEEN
If in the early part of the season, the population of a hive becomes uncomfortably crowded as the bees make preparations for swarming. A number of royal cells are constructed, and they are always almost placed upon those edges of the combs that are not attached to the sides of the hive. These cells resemble a small peanut, about an inch deep and one-third of an inch in diameter. They are very thick and require a large quantity of material for their construction. These cells are seldom seen in a perfect state, as the bees nibble them away after the Queen has hatched, leaving only their remains in the shape of a very small acorn-cup.

While the other cells open sideways, these always hang with their mouth downwards. Much speculation has arisen as to the reason for this deviation: Some conjecture that their peculiar position exerted an influence upon the development of the royal larvae; while others, having ascertained that no injurious effect was produced by turning them upwards, or placing them in any other position, have considered this deviation as among the inscrutable mysteries of the beehive. So it always seemed to me, until more careful reflection enabled me to solve the problem. The Queen cells open downwards, simply *to save room*! The distance between the parallel ranges of comb being usually less than half an inch, the bees could not have made the royal cells to open sideways, without sacrificing the cells opposite to them. In order to economize space, to the very utmost, they put them upon the unoccupied edges of the comb, as the only place where there is always plenty of room for such very large cells.

The number of royal cells varies greatly; sometimes there are only two or three, ordinarily there are five or six, and I have occasionally seen more than a dozen. They are not all commenced at once, for the bees do not intend that the young Queens shall all arrive at maturity at the same time. In some few instances, I have known the bees to transfer the eggs from common to Queen cells, and this *may* be their general method of procedure. I shall hazard the conjecture that the Queen deposits her eggs in cells on the edges of the comb, in a crowded state of the hive, and that some of these are afterwards enlarged and changed into royal cells by the Workers. Such is the instinctive hatred of the Queen to her own kind, that it does not seem to me probable that she is entrusted with even the initiatory steps for securing a race of successors. That the eggs from which the young Queens are produced, are of the same kind with those producing Workers, has been repeatedly demonstrated. On examining the Queen cells while they are in progress, one of the first things that catches our notice is the very unusual amount of attention bestowed upon them by the Workers. There is scarcely a second in which a bee is not peeping into them, and just as fast as one is satisfied, another pops its head in, to examine if not to report, progress. The importance of their inmates to the bee community might easily be inferred from their being the center of so much attraction.

ROYAL JELLY

The young Queens are supplied with a much larger quantity of food than is allotted to the other larvae, so that they seem almost to float in a thick bed of jelly, and there is usually a portion of it left unconsumed at the base of the cells, after the insects have arrived at maturity. It is different from the food of either Drones or Workers, and in appearance, resembles a light quince jelly, having a slightly acid taste.

The effects produced upon the larvae by this peculiar food and method of treatment, are very remarkable. The most important of these effects, I shall now enumerate:

1. The peculiar manner in which the worm designed to be reared as a Queen is treated causes it to arrive at maturity about one-third earlier than if it had been bred a Worker. And yet it is much more fully developed.

2. Its organs of reproduction are completely developed, so that it is capable of fulfilling the role of a mother.

3. Its size, shape and color are all greatly changed. Its lower jaws are shorter, its head rounder, and its legs have neither brushes nor baskets, while its stinger is more curved, and one-third longer than that of a Worker.

4. Its *instincts* are entirely changed. Reared as a Worker, it would have been ready to thrust out its stinger

upon the least provocation; whereas now it may be pulled limb from limb without even attempting to sting. As a Worker it would have treated a Queen with the greatest consideration; whereas now, if placed under a glass with another Queen, it rushes forthwith to mortal combat with its rival. As a Worker, it would frequently have left the hive, either for labor or exercise: as a Queen, after impregnation, it never leaves the hive except to accompany a new swarm.

5. The term of its life is remarkably lengthened. As a Worker, it would have lived not more than six or seven months at farthest; as a Queen it may live seven or eight times as long!

ARTIFICIAL REARING OF QUEENS

The distress of the bees when they lose their Queen is great. If they have the means of replacing her loss, they soon calm down and commence rearing another. The process of rearing Queens artificially to meet some special emergency is even more wondrous than the natural one. Its success depends on the bees having Worker-eggs or worms not more than three days old; if older, the larva has been too far developed as a Worker to allow any change.

The bees nibble away the partitions of two cells adjoining a third, so as to make one large cell out of the three. They destroy the eggs or worms in two of these cells, while they place before the occupant of the third the usual food of the young Queens, and build out its cell to give it ample space for development.

They do not attempt to rear a single Queen, but to guard against failure start producing a considerable number, although the work on all but a few is usually soon discontinued.

In twelve or fourteen days, they are in possession of a new Queen, similar to one reared in the natural way.

NATURAL INDUSTRY

Industry belongs to the bees' nature. When the flowers yield honey, and the weather is fine, they need no encouragement from man to perform their part. When their tenement is supplied with all things necessary to reach another spring, or their storehouse full, and we supply them with more space, they will assiduously toil to fill it up.

Basics of ... Beekeeping

Ancient cave painting at Cuevas de la Araña in Spain depicting honey collection.

CHAPTER TWO

A BRIEF HISTORY OF BEEKEEPING

Our ancestors began collecting honey at least 8,000 years ago, as evidenced by a cave painting at Cuevas de la Araña (Spider Caves) in Valencia, Spain. This Mesolithic rock painting shows two hunters collecting honey and honeycomb from a wild bee nest. The figures are depicted carrying baskets and using a ladder to reach the honey.

The oldest remains of honey have been found in Georgia, in the Caucasus region of Eurasia. Archaeologists have detected honey on the inner surface of clay vessels unearthed in an ancient tomb that dates back some 5,500 years ago. Honey was stored for the dead's journey into the afterlife.

In ancient Egypt, honey was used to sweeten cakes and biscuits. Honey was used as an offering to Min, the fertility god of Egypt. Ancient Egyptians and Middle Easterners also used honey in embalming the dead. Sealed pots of honey have been found in the tombs of Tutankhamen and other Egyptian pharaohs.

The spiritual and therapeutic use of honey is recorded in the 4,000-year-old Vedas and Ayurveda texts of ancient India. In Hinduism, honey was one of the five elixirs of immortality. It was poured of statues of deities in a ceremony called *Madhu Abhisheka* (honey prayer ritual).

Pliny the Elder wrote about honeybees in his *Naturalis Historia*. Roman authors Athenaeus, Cato, and

Basics of ... Beekeeping

Bassus noted honey's use as a sweetener in food. Some of these recipes are collected in the book *Roman Cookery*.

In the ancient Chinese text *Golden Rules of Business Success* by Fan Li (or Tao Zhu Gong), there is the mention of beekeeping.

In South America, the Maya cultivated a stingless bee for its honey.

In Africa and Asia, the Honeyguide bird (family: *Indicatoridae*) has been used for centuries to locate honey. These birds deliberately lead humans to bee colonies, so that they can feast on the grubs and beeswax left behind.

Collecting honey from wild bee colonies is still practiced by aboriginal societies in parts of Africa, Asia, Australia, and South America.

Beekeeping developed as early humans learned how to domesticate bees using artificial hives made from hollow logs, wooden boxes, pottery vessels, and woven straw baskets called "skeps."

In the 8th Century BCE, Shamash-resh-u ur, the governor of Suhu tried to introduce beekeeping into Mesopotamia. The story was recorded on a stele:

> "Bees that collect honey, which none of my ancestors had ever seen or brought into the land of Suhu, I brought down from the mountain of the men of Habha, and made them settle in the orchards of the town 'Gabbari-built-it.' They collect honey and wax, and I know how to melt the honey and wax – and the gardeners know too."

During the Medieval period, abbeys and monasteries

were traditionally centers for beekeeping. Monks became expert at producing honey for the monastery's consumption.

Beekeeping in the 16th Century.

By the 18th century European naturalists began the scientific study of bee colonies and the complex world of bee biology. Notable among them were Dutch biologist Jan Swammerdam, French ethologist René Antoine Ferchault de Réaumur, Swiss naturalist Charles Bonnet, and the blind Swiss scientist François Huber.

The transition from old beekeeping to the new was documented in the works of Thomas Wildman. His book – *A Treatise on the Management of Bees; Wherin is contained the Natural History of those Insects; with the various methods of cultivating them, both Antient and Modern, and the improved Treatment of them. To which are added the Natural History of Wasps and Hornets, and the means of destroying them* – was published in London in 1768.

Wildman advocated beekeeping using the Warré hive.

Wildman's hive elements are made like skeps, only open at the top. Round the top ring of straw is a wooden hoop on which to rest the top-bars. There are 5 main top-bars and two narrower and shorter ones at the sides. The elements are 7.5 inches (190 mm) high and 10 inches (254 mm) internal diameter. The top bars are a quarter of an inch (6.35 mm) deep and one and a quarter inches (32 mm) wide. There is a gap of half an inch (13 mm) between adjacent bars. Initially, two elements of the hive are populated.

The 19th century saw this revolution in beekeeping completed through the perfection of the movable comb hive. American beekeeper Lorenzo Lorraine Langstroth (a contributor to this guidebook) perfected the movable comb hive by applying Huber's discovery that there was a specific spatial measurement between the wax combs in a hive.

No other individual has influenced modern beekeeping practice more than L.L. Langstroth. Today he is revered as the "father of American apiculture."

Basics of ... Beekeeping

CHAPTER THREE

APICULTURE

The scientific term for beekeeping is *apiculture*.

A beekeeper (or *apiarist*) keeps bees in order to collect their honey, to pollinate crops, or to sell bees to other beekeepers.

The location where bees are kept is known as an *apiary*, or "bee yard."

TRADITIONAL BEEKEEPING

Traditional Beekeeping relied on a fixed comb hive. That's a hive in which the combs cannot be removed or manipulated for management or harvesting without permanently damaging the comb. These include log gums, skeps, baskets, and clay pots. However, this type of hive is no longer common in industrialized countries.

Fixed comb hives.

Basics of ... Beekeeping

BEE GUMS

In the southeastern United States, southeast, sections of hollow trees were used as hives for harvesting honey. These were called "gums" because they often were created from black gum trees (*Nyssa sylvatica*).

MODERN BEEKEEPING

Modern Beekeeping relies on movable frame hives, where honeycombs can be removed without damage. In the United States, the Langstroth Hive is prevalent. This was the first successful top-opened hive with movable frames, and most other designs are based on it. (Note: Lorenzo Lorraine Langstroth was one of the contributors to this volume.)

L.L. Langstroth   The Langstroth Hive

In the UK the British National Hive is more commonly used, conforming to certain standard frame designs.

TOP-BAR HIVE

An increasing number of beekeepers are adopting the Top-Bar Hive, based on an African design. This style was also used in Greece and Vietnam. Here the hive has no frames and the comb is not returned to the hive after extraction (as with the Langstroth Hive). Because of its lower production, the Top-Bar Hive is favored mainly by people interested in having bees in their garden rather than gathering honey.

Top-Bar Designs

NATURAL BEEKEEPING

There is a Natural Beekeeping Movement that opposes many modern agricultural practices such as hive movement and inspections, routine medication, crop spraying, and sugar water feeding. They believe these things weaken beehives. Much of this can attributed to the 2007 publication of *The Barefoot Beekeeper* by Philip Chandler, a tome that challenged many aspects of Modern Beekeeping and favored the Horizontal Top-bar Hive.

Basics of ... Beekeeping

URBAN BEEKEEPING

Urban Beekeeping is a growing trend toward the use of small-scale colonies to pollinate personal gardens. These homeowners often help feed their bees by planting flowers that provide nectar and pollen. Some studies have found that "city bees" are healthier than "rural bees" because they encounter fewer pesticides in urban settings.

BEEKEEPER'S GARB

Most beekeepers wear protective clothing, usually a thick suit with hat and veil. Novice beekeepers usually wear gloves, but the more experienced prefer to have their hands free for delicate manipulations.

The protective bee suit is generally made of a light-

Lorenzo Lorraine Langstroth

colored, smooth material. The veil is important since defensive bees are attracted to the breath. A sting on the face can be particularly painful.

Basics of ... Beekeeping

CHAPTER FOUR

HONEY AND POLLEN

As the childhood poem describes it:

How doth the little busy bee
Improve each shining hour,
And gather honey all the day
From every opening flower.

Worker bees collect nectar from flowering plants. Back in the hive, they use their "honey stomachs" to ingest and regurgitate the nectar a number of times until it is partially digested. An enzyme known as *invertase* is synthesized by the bees. This enzyme is combined with digestive acids to hydrolyze the nectar's sucrose into a mixture of glucose and fructose. This process of regurgitation and evaporation produces the substance we know as honey.

HONEYCOMB

Bees manufacture honey as a food source. They store it in wax honeycombs inside the beehive. Workers construct these hexagonal cells of wax for the express purpose of storing honey and eggs. Beekeepers harvest the excess honey for our own tables.

Honey has about the same sweetness as granulated sugar. This sweetness comes from the properties of the monosaccharaides fructose and glucose.

Honey is the only food in nature that will not spoil.

Because its natural sugars are dehydrated, a quality which prevents fermentation, a jar of honey will remain edible for over 3,000 years.

Most microorganisms do not grow in honey because of its low water activity of 0.6. However, honey sometimes contains dormant endospores of the bacterium *Clostridium botulinum*, which can be dangerous to infants because the endospores can transform into toxin-producing bacteria in immature intestinal tracts.

NECTAR

Nectar is a sugary fluid secreted by plants, especially flowers, to encourage pollination by insects and other animals. It is collected by bees to make into honey.

Although nectar's main ingredient is natural sugar (i.e., sucrose, glucose, and fructose) it is a brew of many chemicals. All 20 of the normal amino acids found in protein have been identified in various nectars, with alanine, arginine, serine, proline, glycine, isoleucine, threonine and valine being the most prevalent.

Floral nectaries are generally located at the base of a flower's perianth, so pollinators are made to brush against the flower's reproductive structures, the anthers and pistil, while accessing the nectar. Insects and birds who eat sugar-rich nectar are called Nectarivores.

POLLEN, OR BEEBREAD

Pollen is a powdery substance discharged from the male part of a flower. Each grain contains a male gamete that can fertilize the flower's female ovule.

This yellowish substance is gathered by the bees from the flowers, or blossoms. These foraging bees bring the pollen back to the hive where it is passed along to other bees who pack it into brood cells using their heads. During the packing, the pollen is mixed with nectar, enzymes, fungi, and bacterial organisms. Then the Queen deposits a single egg on top of the pollen ball before sealing off the cell.

When a colony is actively engaged in carrying pollen, it may be taken for granted that they have a fertile Queen, and are busy breeding. To the contrary, if any colony is not gathering pollen when others are, the Queen is either dead or diseased.

We are indebted to the Swiss naturalist François Huber (1750 - 1831) for the discovery of the use bees make of pollen – mainly, for the nourishment of embryo bees.

GATHERING POLLEN

The bees continue to gather fresh beebread, even when there are large accumulations of old stores in the cells.

The mode of gathering is very interesting. The body of the bee appears, to the naked eye, to be covered with fine hairs. The farina adheres to these when the bee alights on a flower. With her legs, she brushes it off from her body, and packs it in two hollows, or *baskets*, one on each of her thighs. These baskets are surrounded by stouter hairs, which hold the load in its place.

When the bee returns with pollen, she often makes a dancing or vibratory motion which attracts the attention of the other bees, who at once nibble away from her thighs what they want for immediate use; the rest she deposits in a cell for future need, where it is carefully packed down, and sealed over with wax.

It has been observed that when gathering pollen a bee always confines herself to the same kind of flower on which she begins, even when it may not be so abundant as some others.

Thus if you examine a ball of this substance taken from her thigh, it will be one uniform color throughout: the load of one will be yellow, another red, and a third brown. The color varies according to that of the plant from which it was obtained.

BON APPETIT!

Bees are adapted for feeding on nectar and pollen – nectar primarily as an energy source and pollen primarily for protein and other nutrients. Most pollen is used as food for larvae.

Bees have a long proboscis (a complex "tongue") that enables them to obtain the nectar from flowers.

HONEY PRODUCTION

What would be the result in the aggregate of all the honey produced in the flowers of the United States annually? Suppose we estimate the productions of one acre to be one pound of honey (this estimate is probably enough for the average). New York State, for instance, contains 47,000 square miles; 640 acres in a square mile will multiply into a little more than 30,000,000, and each acre producing its pound of honey, we have the grand total of 30,000,000 pounds of honey each year.

PURE HONEY

According to The National Honey Board (a USDA-overseen organization), "Honey stipulates a pure product that does not allow for the addition of any other substance ... this includes, but is not limited to, water or other sweeteners."

HONEY

Honey, when stored in a pint tumbler, just large enough to receive one comb, has a most beautiful appearance, and may be easily taken out whole, and placed in an elegant shape upon the table for dining. Or the honey may be stored indefinitely in jars and used as a sweetener with pancakes and breads and other foods. Honey is also used in cooking, baking, sauces, and as an addition to such beverages as tea. Its exquisite flavor will please the palate. Flavors of honey vary based on the nectar source.

Basics of ... Beekeeping

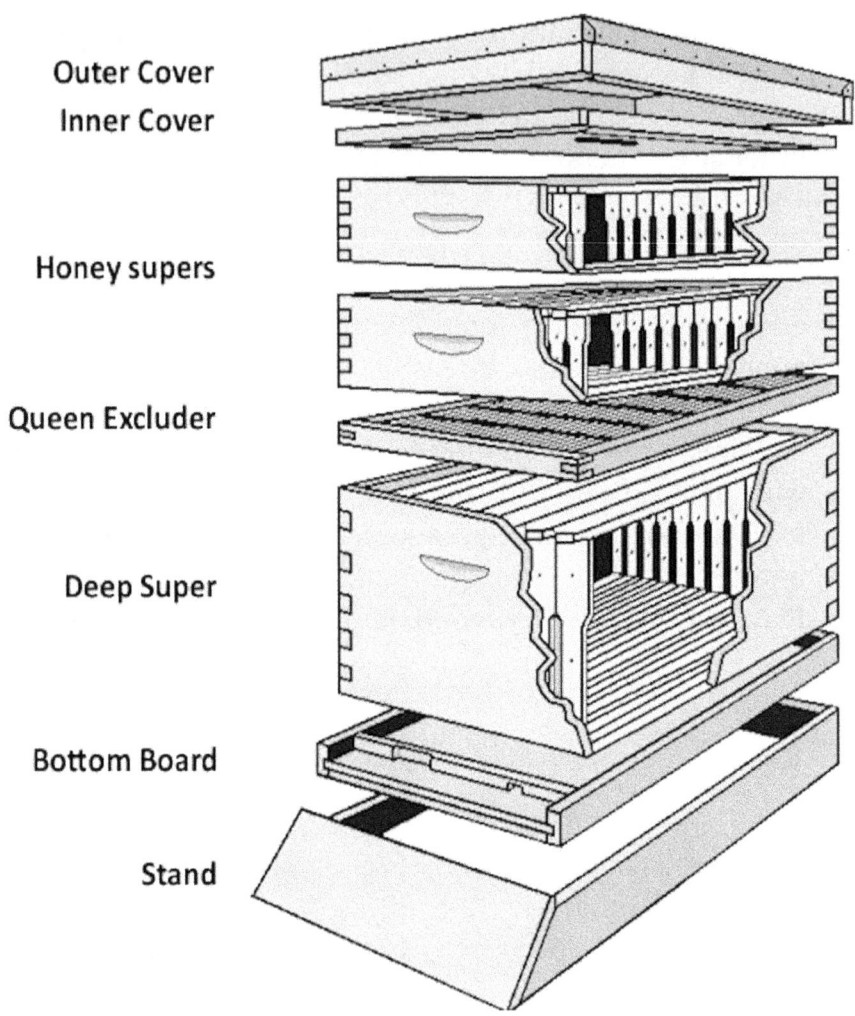

CHAPTER FIVE
THE HIVE

Sectional hives of various patterns have been patented. Such a hive generally consists of three boxes, one above another; the top of each has one large hole, or several small ones, or crossbars, about an inch wide, and half an inch apart.

These holes or spaces allow the bees to pass from one box to the other. When all are full, the upper one is removed, and an empty one put under the bottom; in this way all are changed, and the combs are renewed in three years.

CONSTRUCTION OF THE HIVE

Hives should be constructed of good materials, boards of good thickness, free from flaws and cracks, well fitted and thoroughly nailed.

Even though seeking the cheapest possible construction, a painted hive appears so much nicer to the eye that it ought to be done – especially as the paint adds enough to its durability to pay the expense.

While the color can be whatever your fancy dictates, white is affected the least by the sun in hot weather.

When hives are not painted, the grain should never be crosswise, having the width of boards form the height. Not that the bees would have any dislike to such, but nails will not hold firmly and draw out in a few years.

Construction of a hive should be done ahead of the

Basics of ... Beekeeping

swarming period, because if the hives are to be painted you should do it as long as possible before, because the smell of just-applied oil and paint can prove offensive to the bees.

KIND OF WOOD

While pine is commonly used for building hives, other woods will suffice. Bees do not seem to prefer one kind better than another.

Hemlock is used to a great extent; but is very liable to split after the bees have been in the hive for a time. It should be used only when better wood cannot be obtained.

Basswood when used for hives should always be painted, so it won't warp from moisture arising from the bees inside.

When not painted outside, and allowed to get wet, so much moisture is absorbed that it will bend outward, and separate from the combs and crack them.

Some beekeepers plane the boards for hives inside and out, but produces a problem for bees. When first put into such a hive, they encounter difficulty in holding fast until they get their combs started.

SHAPE OF NO CONSEQUENCE

Boards should be selected, if possible, that will be the proper width to make the hive about square. Say twelve inches square, inside, by fourteen deep. I prefer this shape to any other, yet it is not all that important.

I have had some hives ten inches square by twenty in length; they were awkward looking, but that was all. I could discover no difference in their prosperity.

SIZE OF HIVE

The Queen needs room for all her eggs and the bees need space to store their winter provisions. This should be constructed as one apartment. When too small, their winter supply of food may run out. Also the swarms will be smaller and the stock much more susceptible to accidents.

About the first of April the bees begin collecting pollen and rearing their young; by the middle of May good stocks will occupy nearly all their brood-combs, but little honey can be obtained before fruit blossoms appear. And when these fruit blossoms are gone, no more will be obtained until clover appears, several days later.

If this season of fruit flowers is accompanied by high winds, or cold rainy weather, little honey will be produced. However, our bees have a brood that needs to be fed. If no honey is on hand from the previous year, a famine ensues. When this happens they will mercilessly destroy their Drones and perhaps some of their brood.

Prudence therefore dictates providing for this kind of emergency by making the hive a little larger for northern latitudes, as more honey will be stored to take them through this critical period. You'll find 2,000 inches is a proper size for safety. Swarms from this size hive are on an average as large as any.

THE QUALITIES OF A GOOD HIVE

1. A good hive should give the Apiarian a perfect control over all the combs: so that any of them may be taken out at pleasure; and this, without cutting them, or enraging the bees.

This advantage is possessed by no hive in use, except

my own; and it forms the very foundation of an improved and profitable system of bee-culture. Unless the combs are at the entire command of the Apiarian, he can have no effectual control over his bees. They swarm too much or too little, just as suits themselves, and their owner is almost entirely dependent upon their caprice.

2. It ought to afford suitable protection against extremes of heat and cold, sudden changes of temperature, and the injurious effects of dampness.

In winter, the interior of the hive should be dry, and not a particle of frost should ever find admission; and in summer, the bees should not be forced to work to disadvantage in a pent and almost suffocating heat.

3. It should permit all necessary operations to be performed without hurting or killing a single bee.

Most hives are so constructed that it is impossible to manage them, without at times injuring or destroying some of the bees. The mere destruction of a few bees, would not, except on the score of humanity, be of much consequence, if it did not very materially increase the difficulty of managing them. Bees remember injuries done to any of their number, for some time, and generally find an opportunity to avenge them.

4. It should allow every thing to be done that is necessary in the most extensive management of bees, without incurring any serious risk of exciting their anger.

5. Not a single unnecessary step or motion ought to be required of a single bee.

The honey harvest, in most locations, is of short continuance; and all the arrangements of the hive should facilitate, to the utmost, the work of the busy gatherers.

Tall hives, therefore, and all such as compel them to travel with their heavy burdens through densely crowded combs, are very objectionable. The bees in my hive, instead of forcing their way through thick clusters, can easily pass into the surplus honey boxes, not only from any comb in the hive, but without traveling over the combs at all.

6. It should afford suitable facilities for inspecting, at all times, the condition of the bees.

When the sides of my hive are of glass, as soon as the outer cover is elevated, the apiarian has a view of the interior, and can often at a glance, determine its condition. If the hive is of wood, or if he wishes to make a more thorough examination, in a few minutes every comb may be taken out, and separately inspected. In this way, the exact condition of every colony may always be easily ascertained, and nothing left, as in the common hives, to mere conjecture. This is an advantage, the importance of which it would be difficult to over estimate.

7. While the hive is of a size adapted to the natural instincts of the bee, it should be capable of being readily adjusted to the wants of small colonies.

If a small swarm is put into a large hive, they will be unable to concentrate their animal heat, so as to work to the best advantage, and will often become discouraged, and abandon their hive. If they are put into a small hive, its limited dimensions will not afford them suitable accommodations for increase. By means of my movable partition, my hive can, in a few moments, be adapted to the wants of any colony however small, and can, with equal facility, be enlarged from time to time, or at once restored to its full dimensions.

8. It should allow the combs to be removed without any jarring.

Bees manifest the utmost aversion to any sudden jar; for it is in this way, that their combs are loosened and detached. However firmly fastened the frames may be in my hive, they can all be loosened in a few moments, without injuring or exciting the bees.

9. It should allow every good piece of comb to be given to the bees, instead of being melted into wax.

10. The construction of the hive should induce the bees to build their combs with great regularity.

A hive that contains a large proportion of irregular comb can never be expected to prosper. Such comb is only suitable for storing honey, or raising Drones. This is one reason why so many colonies never flourish. A glance will often show that a hive contains so much Drone comb, as to be unfit for the purposes of a stock hive.

11. It should furnish the means of procuring comb to be used as a guide to the bees, in building regular combs in empty hives; and to induce them more readily to take possession of the surplus honey receptacles.

It is well known that the presence of comb will induce bees to begin work much more readily than they otherwise would: this is especially the case in glass vessels.

12. It should allow the removal of Drone combs from the hive, to prevent the breeding of too many Drones. (See remarks on Drones.)

13. It should enable the apiarian, when the combs become too old, to remove them, and supply their place with new ones.

No hive can, in this respect, equal one in which, in a

few moments, any comb can be removed, and the part which is too old, be cut off. The upper part of a comb, which is generally used for storing honey, will last without renewal for many years.

14. It ought to furnish the greatest possible security against the ravages of the Bee Moth.

Neither before nor after it is occupied, ought there to be any cracks or crevices in the interior. All such places will be filled by the bees with propolis or bee-glue; a substance, which is always soft in the summer heat of the hive, and which forms a most congenial place of deposit for the eggs of the moth.

If the sides of the hive are of glass, and the corners are run with a melted mixture, three parts rosin, and one part bees-wax, the bees will waste but little time in gathering propolis, and the bee-moth will find but little chance for laying her eggs, even if she should succeed in entering the hive.

My hives are so constructed, that if made of wood, they may be thoroughly painted inside and outside, without being so smooth as to annoy the bees; for they travel over the frames to which the combs are attached; and thus whether the inside surface is glass or wood, it is not liable to crack, or warp, or absorb moisture, after the hive is occupied by the bees. If the hives are painted inside, it should be done sometime before they are used. If the interior of the wooden hive is brushed with a very hot mixture of the rosin and bees-wax, the hives may be used immediately.

15. It should furnish some place accessible to the apiarian, where the bee-moth can be tempted to deposit

Basics of ... Beekeeping

her eggs, and the worms, when full grown, to wind themselves in their cocoons.

16. It should enable the apiarian, if the bee moth ever gains the upper hand of the bees, to remove the combs, and expel the worms.

17. The bottom board should be permanently attached to the hive; for if this is not done, it will be inconvenient to move the hive when bees are in it, and next to impossible to prevent the depredations of moths and worms.

Sooner or later, there will be crevices between the bottom board and the sides of the hive, through which the moths will gain admission, and under which the worms, when fully grown, will retreat to spin their webs, and to be changed into moths, to enter in their turn, and lay their eggs. Movable bottom hoards are a great nuisance in the apiary, and the construction of my hive, which enables me entirely to dispense with them, will furnish a very great protection against the bee moth. There is no place where they can get in, except at the entrance for the bees, and this may be contracted or enlarged, to suit the strength of the colony; and from its peculiar shape, the bees are enabled to defend it against intruders, with the greatest advantage.

18. The bottom-board should slant towards the entrance, to assist the bees in carrying out the dead, and other useless substances; to aid them in defending themselves against robbers; to carry off all moisture; and to prevent the rain and snow from beating into the hive. As a farther precaution against this last evil, the entrance ought to be under a covered way, which should not, at once lead into the interior.

19. The bottom-board should be so constructed that it may be readily cleared of dead bees in cold weather, when the bees are unable to attend to this business themselves.

If suffered to remain, they often become moldy, and injure the health of the colony. If the bees drag them out, as they will do, if the weather moderates, they often fall with them on the snow, and are so chilled that they never rise again; for a bee generally retains its hold in flying away with the dead, until both fall to the ground.

20. No part of the interior of the hive should be below the level of the place of exit.

If this principle is violated, the bees must, at great disadvantage, drag their dead, and all the refuse of the hive, *up hill*. Such hives will often have their bottom boards covered with small pieces of comb, beebread, and other impurities, in which the moth delights to lay her eggs; and which furnished her progeny with a most congenial nourishment, until they are able to get access to the combs.

21. It should afford facilities for feeding the bees both in warm and cold weather.

In this respect, my hive has very unusual advantages. Sixty colonies in warm weather may, in an hour, be fed a quart each, and yet no feeder be used, and no risk incurred from robbing bees.

22. It should allow of the easy hiving of a swarm, without injuring any of the bees, or risking the destruction of the Queen.

23. It should admit of the safe transportation of the bees to any distance whatever.

The permanent bottom-board, the firm attachment of

the combs, each to a separate frame, and the facility with which, in my hive, any amount of air can be given to the bees when shut up, most admirably adapt it to this purpose.

24. It should furnish the bees with air when the entrance is shut; and the ventilation for this purpose ought to be unobstructed, even if the hives should be buried in two or three feet of snow.

25. A good hive should furnish facilities for enlarging, contracting, and closing the entrance; so as to protect the bees against robbers, and the bee-moth; and when the entrance is altered, the bees ought not to lose valuable time in searching for it, as they must do in most hives.

26. It should give the bees the means of ventilating their hives, without enlarging the entrance too much, so as to expose them to moths and robbers, and to the risk of losing their brood by a chill in sudden changes of weather.

To secure this end, the ventilators must not only be independent of the entrance, but they must owe their efficiency mainly to the co-operation of the bees themselves, who thus have a free admission of air only when they want it. To depend on the opening and shutting of the ventilators by the beekeeper, is entirely out of the question.

27. It should furnish facilities for admitting at once, a large body of air; so that in winter, or early spring, when the weather is at any time unusually mild, the bees may be tempted to fly out and discharge their feces.

If such a free admission of air cannot be given to hives that are thoroughly protected against the cold, the bees may lose a favorable opportunity of emptying themselves;

and thus be more exposed than they otherwise would, to suffer from diseases resulting from too long confinement. A very free admission of air is also desirable when the weather is exceedingly hot.

28. It should enable the apiarian to remove the excess of beebread from old stocks.

This article always accumulates in old hives, so that in the course of time, many of the combs are filled with it, thus unfitting them for the rearing of brood, and the reception of honey. Young stocks, on the other hand, will often be so deficient in this important article, that in the early part of the season, breeding will be seriously interfered with. By means of my movable frames, the excess of old colonies may be made to supply the deficiency of young ones, to the mutual benefit of both.

29. It should enable the apiarian, when he has removed the combs from a common hive, to place them with the bees, brood, honey and beebread, in the improved hive, so that the bees may be able to attach them in their natural positions.

30. It should allow of the easy and safe dislodgement of the bees from the hive.

This requisite is especially important to secure the union of colonies, when it becomes necessary to break up some of the stocks. (See remarks on the Union of Stocks.)

31. It should allow the heat and odor of the main hive, as well as the bees themselves, to pass in the freest manner, to the surplus honey receptacles.

In this respect, all the hives with which I am acquainted, are more or less deficient: the bees are forced to work in receptacles difficult of access, and in which,

Basics of ... Beekeeping

especially in cool nights, they find it impossible to keep up the animal heat necessary for comb-building. Bees cannot, in such hives, work to advantage in glass tumblers, or other small vessels. One of the most important arrangements of my hive is that by which the heat ascends into all the receptacles for storing honey, as naturally and almost as easily as the warmest air ascends to the top of a heated room.

32. It should permit the surplus honey to be taken away, in the most convenient, beautiful and salable forms, at any time, and without any risk of annoyance from the bees.

In my hives, it may be taken in tumblers, glass boxes, wooden boxes small or large, earthen jars, flower-pots; in short, in any kind of receptacle which may suit the fancy, or the convenience of the beekeeper. Or all these may be dispensed with, and the honey may be taken from the interior of the main hive, by removing the frames with loaded combs, and supplying their place with empty ones.

33. It should admit of the easy removal of all the good honey from the main hive, that its place might be supplied with an inferior article. Bee-Keepers who have but few colonies, and who wish to secure the largest yield, may remove the loaded combs from my hive, slice off the covers of the cells, drain out the honey, and restore the empty combs, into which, if the season of gathering is over, they can first pour the cheap foreign honey for the use of the bees.

34. It should allow, when quantity not quality is the object, the largest amount of honey to be gathered; so that the surplus of strong colonies may, in the fall, be given to

those which have not a sufficient supply.

By surmounting my hive with a box of the same dimensions, the combs may all be transferred to this box, and the bees, when they commence building, will descend and fill the lower frames, gradually using the upper box, as the brood is hatched out, for storing honey. In this way, the largest possible yield of honey may be secured, as the bees always prefer to continue their work below, rather than above the main hive, and will never swarm, when allowed in season, ample room in this direction. The combs in the upper box, containing a large amount of beebread and being of a size adapted to the breeding of Workers, will be all the better for aiding weak colonies.

35. It should compel, when desired, the force of the colony to be mainly directed to raising young bees; so that brood may be on hand to form new colonies, and strengthen feeble stocks.

36. It ought, while well protected from the weather, to be so constructed, that in warm, sunny days in early spring, the influence of the sun may be allowed to penetrate and warm up the hive, so as to encourage early breeding.

37. The hive should be equally well adapted to be used as a swarmer, or non-swarmer.

Non-swarming hives managed in the ordinary way are liable, in spite of all precautions, to swarm very unexpectedly, and if not closely watched, the swarm is lost, and with it the profit of that season. By having the command of the combs, the Queen in my hives can always be caught and deprived of her wings; thus she cannot go off with a swarm, and they will not leave without her.

38. It should enable the apiarian, if he allows his bees

Basics of ... Beekeeping

to swarm, and wishes to secure surplus honey, to prevent them from throwing more than one swarm in a season.

Second and third swarms must be returned to the old stock, if the largest quantities of surplus honey are to be realized. It is troublesome to watch them, deprive them of their Queens, and restore them to the parent hive. They often issue with new Queens again and again; and waste, in this way, both their own time, and that of their keeper. "An ounce of prevention is worth a pound of cure." In my hives, as soon as the first swarm has issued, and been hived, all the Queen cells except one, in the hive from which it came, may be cut out, and thus all after-swarming will very easily and effectually be prevented. When the old stock is left with but one Queen, she runs no risk of being killed or crippled in a contest with rivals. By such contests, a colony is often left without a Queen, or in possession of one that is too much maimed to be of any service.

39. A good hive should enable the apiarian, if he relies on natural swarming, and wishes to multiply his colonies as fast as possible, to make vigorous stocks of all his small after-swarms.

Such swarms contain a young Queen, and if they can be judiciously strengthened, usually make the best stock hives. If hived in a common hive, and left to themselves, unless very early, or in very favorable seasons, they seldom thrive. They generally desert their hives, or perish in the winter. If they are small, they cannot be made powerful, even by the most generous feeding. There are too few bees to build comb, and take care of the eggs which a healthy Queen can lay; and when fed, they are apt to fill with honey, the cells in which young bees ought to be raised;

thus making the kindness of their owner serve only to hasten their destruction. My hives enable me to supply all such swarms at once with combs containing beebread, honey and brood almost mature. They are thus made strong, and flourish as well, nay, often better than the first swarms which have an old Queen, whose fertility is generally not so great as that of a young one.

40. It should enable the apiarian to multiply his colonies with a certainty and rapidity that are entirely out of the question, if he depends upon natural swarming.

41. It should enable the apiarian to supply destitute colonies with the means of obtaining a new Queen.

Every apiarian would find it, for this reason, if for no other, to his advantage to possess, at least, one such hive.

42. It should enable him to catch the Queen, for any purpose; especially to remove an old one whose fertility is impaired by age that her place may be supplied with a young one.

43. While a good hive is adapted to the wants of those who desire to enter upon beekeeping on a large scale, or at least to manage their colonies on the most improved plans, it ought to be suited to the wants of those who are too timid, too ignorant, or for any reason indisposed, to manage them in any other than the common way.

44. It should enable a single individual to superintend the colonies of many different persons.

Many would like to keep bees, if they could have them taken care of, by those who would undertake their management, just as a gardener does the gardens and grounds of his employers. No person can agree to do this with the common hives. If the bees are allowed to swarm, he may be called in a dozen different directions, and if any accident, such as the loss of a Queen, happens to the colonies of his customers, he can apply no remedy. If the bees are in non-swarming hives, he cannot multiply the stocks when this is desired.

On my plan, gentlemen who desire it, may have the pleasure of witnessing the industry and sagacity of this wonderful insect, and of gratifying their palates with its delicious stores, harvested on their own premises, without incurring either trouble or risk of injury.

45. All the joints of the hive should be watertight, and there should be no doors or slides that are liable to shrink, swell, or get out of order.

The importance of this will be sufficiently obvious to anyone who has had the ordinary share of vexatious experience in the use of such fixtures.

46. It should enable the beekeeper entirely to dispense with sheds, and costly apiaries; as each hive when properly placed, should alike defy, heat or cold, rain or snow.

47. It should allow the contents of a hive, bees, combs and all, to be taken out; so that any necessary repairs may be made.

This may be done, with my hives, in a few minutes. "A stitch in time saves nine." Hives that can be thoroughly overhauled and repaired, from time to time, if properly attended to, will last for generations.

48. The hive and fixtures should present a neat and attractive appearance, and should admit, when desired, of being made highly ornamental.

49. The hives ought not to be liable to be blown down in high winds.

My hives, being very low in proportion to their other dimensions, it would require almost a hurricane to upset them.

50. It should enable an apiarian who lives in the neighborhood of human pilferers, to lock up the precious contents of his hives, in some cheap, simple and convenient way.

A couple of padlocks with some cheap fixtures will suffice to secure a long range of hives.

51. A good hive should be protected against the destructive ravages of mice in winter.

It seems almost incredible that so puny an animal should dare to invade a hive of bees; and yet not infrequently they slip in when the bees are compelled by the cold to retreat from the entrance. Having once found admission, they build themselves a nest in their comfortable abode, eat up the honey, and such bees as are too much chilled to make any resistance; and fill the premises with such an abominable stench, that on the approach of warm weather, the bees often in a body abandon their desecrated home. As soon as the cold weather approaches, all my hives may have their entrances either entirely closed, or so contracted that a mouse cannot gain admission.

52. A good hive should have its alighting board constructed so as to shelter the bees against wind and wet, and thus to facilitate to the utmost their entrance when they come home with their heavy burdens.

If this precaution is neglected, much valuable time and many lives will be sacrificed, as the colony cannot be encouraged to use to the best advantage the unpromising days which so often occur in the working season.

I have succeeded in arranging my alighting board in such a manner that the bees are sheltered against wind and wet, and are able to enter the hive with the least possible loss of time.

53. A well-constructed hive ought to admit of being shut up in winter, so as to consign the bees to darkness and repose.

Nothing can be more hazardous than to shut up closely an ill protected hive. Even if the bees have an abundance of air, it will not answer to prevent them from flying out, if they are so disposed. As soon as the warmth penetrating their thin hives tempts them to fly, they crowd to the entrance, and if it is shut, multitudes worry themselves to death in trying to get out, and the whole colony is liable to become diseased.

In my hives as soon as the bees are shut up for winter, they are most effectually protected against all atmospheric changes, and never *desire* to leave their hives until the entrances are again opened, on the return of suitable weather. Thus they pass the winter in a state of almost absolute repose; they eat much less honey than when wintered on the ordinary plan; a much smaller number die in the hives; none are lost upon the snow, and they are more healthy, and commence breeding much earlier than they do in the common hives. As some of the holes into the Protector are left open in winter, any bee that is diseased and wishes to leave the hive can do so. Bees when diseased have a strange propensity to leave their hives, just as animals when sick seek to retreat from their companions; and in summer such bees may often be seen forsaking their home to perish on the ground. If all egress from the hive in winter is prevented, the diseased bees will not be able to comply with an instinct that urges them "To leave their country for their country's good."

54. It should possess all these requisites without being too costly for common beekeepers, or too complicated to be constructed by anyone who can handle simple tools: and they should be so combined that the result is a simple hive, which anyone can manage who has ordinary intelligence on the subject of bees.

A hive of the simplest possible construction is only a close imitation of the abode of bees in a state of nature; being a mere hollow receptacle in which they are protected from the weather, and where they can lay up their stores.

An improved hive is one which contains, in addition, a separate apartment in which the bees can be induced to lay up the surplus portion of their stores, for the use of their owner. All the various hives in common use, are only modifications of this latter hive, and, as a general rule, they are bad, exactly in proportion as they depart from it. Not one of them offers any remedy for the loss of the Queen, or indeed for most of the casualties to which bees are exposed: they form no reliable basis for any new system of management; and hence the cultivation of bees, is substantially where it was, fifty years ago, and the apiarian as entirely dependent as ever, upon all the whims and caprices of an insect which may be made completely subject to his control.

No hive that does not furnish a thorough control over every comb can be considered as any substantial advance on the simple improved or chamber hive. Of all such hives, the one that with the least expense gives the greatest amount of protection, and the readiest access to the spare honey boxes is the best.

Having thus enumerated the tests to which all hives ought to be subjected, and by which they should stand or fall, I submit them to the candid examination of practical, common sense beekeepers, who have had the largest experience in the management of bees, and are most conversant with the evils of the present system; and who are therefore best fitted to apply them to an invention, which, if I may be pardoned for using the enthusiastic language of an experienced apiarian on examining its practical workings, "introduces, not simply an *improvement*, but a *revolution* in beekeeping."

Basics of ... Beekeeping

Home Sweet Home.

CHAPTER SIX

THE APIARY

In placing the apiary, make sure it is convenient to observe during the swarming season, so as to alert the beekeeper when a swarm rises. Also, the hives should stand where the wind will have little effect, especially from the northwest.

When the hive stands in a bleak place, the bees returning with heavy loads in a high wind are frequently unable to strike the hive, and are blown to the ground, become chilled, and die. A chilly south wind is equally fatal, but not so frequent.

If no hills or buildings offer protection, a high board fence should be put up. It is good economy to do this in that enough bees may be saved to pay the expense. When protected from winds, the hives may front any direction you choose; although east or south is generally preferred.

A location near ponds, lakes, or large rivers will cause some loss. Hard winds can fatigue bees on the wing, causing them to alight in the water. Here they find it impossible to rise until wafted ashore, and by then they are too chilled to survive.

NEEDED BODY HEAT

During the first spring months the stocks contain fewer bees than during any other season. This is when a large family proves to be important, creating the animal heat needed to rear the brood. One bee is of more consequence at that time than a half dozen in midsummer.

Basics of ... Beekeeping

DECIDE LOCATION EARLY

The location of your hives should be decided upon early in the spring, because when the chilling winter winds cease for a day the bees that have been inactive for months will come out to enjoy the balmy air. As they exit the hive, they pause for a moment to rub their eyes, which have long been obscured in darkness.

BEES MARK THEIR LOCATION ON LEAVING THE HIVE

They rise on the wing, but do not leave in a direct line. Immediately they turn their heads towards the entrance of their tenement, describing a circle of only a few inches at first, but enlarge it as they recede, until an area of several yards has been *viewed and marked*.

CHANGING A STAND CREATES LOSS

After a few excursions, when surrounding objects have become familiar, the bees no longer take this marking action. Now they leave in a direct line for their destination and return by their way-marks without difficulty.

Many people assume the bee knows its hive by some kind of instinct, or is attracted towards it, like steel to a magnet. However, their return flight is due to this mapping.

It's a mistake for the beekeeper to move their hives a few yards after the location is thus marked because it can cause confusion, resulting in a materialistic loss of bees.

Let us trace the cause. As I explained, the bees have marked the location. They leave the hive without any precaution because the surrounding objects are now familiar. They return to their old stand and find no home. If there is more than one stock, and the removal has been from four to twenty feet, some of the bees may find their way to a new hive, but are liable to be killed, which is generally the case when a strange bee enters another hive.

SPACE BETWEEN HIVES

As regards the distance between hives, let it be as great as convenience will allow. Want of room makes it necessary sometimes to set them close. But keep in mind, whenever economy of space dictates less than two feet, bees are often lost from entering the wrong hive.

SOME ADVANTAGE IN BEING NEAR THE EARTH

I go counter to some apiarians in recommending that stands be near the earth; less than two or three feet between the bees and the ground.

Now let us compare advantages and disadvantages:

One hive or a row of hives suspended, or standing on a bench, two or three feet from the earth, when approached by the bees on a chilly afternoon (and we have many such in spring), even if there is not much wind, can cause a bee to miss the hive and bottom, and fall to the ground, so numbed with cold as to be unable to rise again, and by the next morning are "no use" whatever.

On the other hand, if the hives are near the earth, with a board as described, there is no *possibility* of their alighting under the hive, and if they should come short and land on the ground they can always creep long after

Basics of ... Beekeeping

they are too cold to fly and enter the hive without the necessity of using their wings.

Examine minutely the earth about your hives, towards sunset on a day in April, when the day has been fair, with some wind, and chilly towards night, and you will be astonished at the numbers of bees that perish. Most of them will be found loaded with pollen, proving them martyrs to their own industry and your negligence.

VENTILATION OF THE HIVE

Pure air is necessary for the respiration of the mature bees. And without proper ventilation, the eggs cannot be hatched or larvae developed.

On warm summer days, bees can become excessively heated, and the combs may melt down. To avoid this, a considerable number of bees will be found standing on the alighting board, with their heads turned towards the entrance, the extremity of their bodies slightly elevated, and their wings in rapid motion to create a brisk current of air. These bees are *ventilating* the hive.

This requires great physical exertion on the part of the bees. And if you watch carefully, you will find that, from time to time, exhausted bees are relieved by fresh detachments.

MOVABLE FRAMES

Each comb in these hives is attached to a movable frame, and they all admit of easy removal. In this respect the construction of the hive is entirely new, and while it greatly facilitates the business of observation, it enables the apiarian, on the approach of cool weather, to transfer his bees from a hive in which they cannot winter, to one of the common construction. As soon as the weather in the spring is sufficiently warm, they may again be placed in the observing hive, in which, (as both sides of every comb admit of inspection,) every bee can be seen, and all the wonders of the hive are exposed to the full light of day. In the common observing hives experiments are often conducted with great difficulty, by cutting away parts of the comb, whereas in mine, they can all be performed by the simple removal of one of the frames, and if the colony becomes reduced in numbers, it may, in a few moments, be strengthened by helping it to maturing brood from one of the other hives.

The first combs built by a swarm are for brood, and store-combs afterwards, as needed; one apartment will be nearly filled with all brood-combs, and the other with store-combs and honey.

Now in the two kinds of cells there is a great difference; those for breeding are near half an inch in length, while those for storing are sometimes two inches or more; totally unfit for breeding; until the bees cut them off to the proper length, which they will not do, unless compelled for want of room, consequently this side of store-combs is but little used for brood. When such hive is divided, the chances are not more than one in four, that this apartment will have any young bees of the proper age from which to raise a Queen; if not, and the old Queen is in the part with the brood-comb, where she will be ninety-nine times in a hundred, one half of the hive is lost for want of a Queen.

SWARMERS VS. NON-SWARMERS

Let's discuss the advantage of swarming hives over non-swarmers. The merit of having a hive is to obtain surplus honey with little trouble, so let's examine it on the score of profit. Suppose we start with one hive, call it worth five dollars in the beginning, at the end of ten years it is worth no more, very likely not as much, (the chances of its failing, short of that time, we will not take into the account;) we might get annually, say five dollars worth of surplus honey, amounting to fifty dollars.

The swarming hive will throw off one swarm annually, and make us one dollar's worth of surplus honey, (we will not reckon that yielded by the first swarm, which is often more than that from the old stocks,) about one third of the average in good seasons. The second year there will be two to do the same; take this rate for ten years, we have 512 stocks, either of them worth as much as the non-swarmer, and about a thousand dollars worth of surplus honey. Call these stocks worth five dollars each, which makes $2,560, all added together will make the snug little sum of about $3,500, against $55. It is not to be expected that any of us will realize profits to this extent, but it is a forcible illustration of the advantages of the swarming hive over the non-swarmer.

FORCING A SWARM

But many of these non-swarmer hives, 'tis said, can be changed to swarmers to suit the convenience of the apiarian. It is asserted that it can be made to swarm within two days at any time, merely by taking off the boxes or drawers. This contracts the room, forcing the bees out.

Basics of ... Beekeeping

Beekeeper.

CHAPTER SEVEN

IRRITABILITY OF BEES

The sting of a bee often produces very painful and, upon some persons, very dangerous effects.

That's why we want to avoid stings.

So how do we keep bees good-natured? It seems rather absurd to think we can teach a *bee* anything! Nevertheless, if we understand the bees' nature, we can usually coerce them to perform to our (safe) specifications.

In the same way that bad training can turn horses or dogs vicious, not understanding how to handle bees can make them ten times more irritable than you might normally expect.

That said, it's better to be safe than sorry.

PROTECTIVE BEE SUIT

Timid apiarians, as well as those allergic to stings, should protect themselves with a bee suit. This is an outfit designed to shield the beekeeper from stings.

It usually consists of a full-body suit and a hat with a veil.

The great objection to gauze-wire veils is that they obstruct a beekeeper's clear vision. And the protective suit tends to generate excessive heat and perspiration, which can be peculiarly offensive to bees.

I prefer to use a bee-hat made of wire cloth, the mesh too fine to admit a bee, but coarse enough to permit the circulation of air. Thick clothing can substitute for the traditional HAZMAT-like beekeepers body suit. Woolen stockings may then be drawn over the hands, or better still, rubber gloves that are impenetrable to the sting of a bee, yet soft and pliant.

Many apiarians dispense with this attire, even at the cost of an occasional sting.

MEANS OF DEFENSE

Every Worker bee is armed with a formidable stinger. When provoked, she makes instant and effectual use of her natural weapon.

The stinger, when subjected to microscopic examination, exhibits a very curious and complicated mechanism. "It is moved by muscles which, though invisible to the eye, are yet strong enough to force the sting to the depth of one twelfth of an inch through the thick skin of a man's hand. At its root are situated two glands by which the poison is secreted: these glands, uniting in one duct, eject the venomous liquid along the groove formed by the junction of the two piercers.

There are four barbs on the outside of each piercer, so when the insect stings one of these piercers, having a point longer than the other darts into the flesh, and then the other strikes in also. The piercer alternately penetrate deeper and deeper till they acquire a firm hold of the flesh with their barbed hooks, and then follows a sheath emptying the poison into the wound.

With the extremity of the stinger being barbed like an arrow, the bee cannot withdraw it. Thus, in losing her stinger she parts with a portion of her intestines, and soon perishes.

Lorenzo Lorraine Langstroth

As the loss of the stinger is always fatal to the bees, they pay a dear penalty for exercising their protective instincts. Nonetheless, bees never hesitate (except when gorged with honey) to die in defense of their home and treasures.

Or as the poet expressed it, they:

*"Deem life itself to vengeance well resign'd,
Die on the wound, and leave their sting behind."*

Note: Hornets, wasps and other stinging insects are able to withdraw their stingers from the wound.

TIME OF GREATEST IRRITABILITY

The season for greatest caution is August. It is then their stores are greatest. At that time a great many things are irritants that in other days might pass unnoticed. It behooves us, therefore, to ascertain what bees consider to be insults.

Basics of ... Beekeeping

PROPER CONDUCT

First, all quick motions, such as running, swatting, etc., are viewed as threatening. If our movements among them are slow, cautious, and respectful, we are often allowed to pass unmolested.

Yet the exhalations of breath from some persons seem to be offensive, for they attack them quicker than others. Whenever a sting occurs, it is perceived at some distance by other bees, which immediately approach the scene to join the attack.

HOW TO PROCEED WHEN ATTACKED

Striking at them only makes them more furious. Not in the least daunted, they return to the attack.

It is best to walk as quietly as possible to the shelter of some bush, or to a house. They will seldom go inside a door.

A PERSON'S BREATH OFFENSIVE

The breath of a person inside the hive, or among bees clustered outside, is considered a great indignity.

A sudden jar, sometimes made by carelessly opening up the hive, is another.

After being irritated in this way, they seem to remember it for weeks, remaining on the alert.

MANNER OF ATTACK

Bees don't always give a warning before stinging – with some attacks the first intimation being the "blow."

At other times, when fully determined on vengeance, I

have had them strike my hat and remain a moment endeavoring to affect their mission. In these cases, I hold down my face to protect it from the next attempt, which is quite sure to follow.

When not so thoroughly charged with anger, they often approach in merely a threatening attitude, buzzing around very provokingly for several minutes in close proximity to my ears and face, apparently to ascertain my intentions. If nothing hostile or displeasing is perceived, they will generally leave; but should a quick motion or offensive breath offend them, the dreaded result is almost sure to follow.

Too many people take these threatening manifestations as positive intentions to sting. When these things can be quietly endured, and at the same time leave their vicinity, it generally ends peaceably.

They never make an attack while away from their home in quest of honey, or on their return, until they have entered the hive. It is only in the hive and its vicinity that we expect to meet this irascible temperament, which should not be allowed, or at least may be subdued in a great measure by doing things in a quiet manner or by the use of tobacco smoke. Any person keeping bees should go armed with this powerful weapon.

USE OF TOBACCO SMOKE

Tobacco smoke is a powerful agent. Some apiarians call it "the grand secret of success."

There is no difficulty working with a sectional or changeable hive, when using a smoker. The combs will be made in the two drawers similar to the dividing hive,

Basics of ... Beekeeping

brood-combs in one side, and store-combs in the other. We wish to remove the one with brood-combs, of course, (as that is the one where the combs are thick and bad, etc.) Where will the Queen be? With the brood-comb, for that is where her duty lies. Well, this is the one we want, and we take it out. But she must go back, or we risk losing the stock. With a smoker her majesty will remain perfectly easy, along with the Workers, no matter where you put the drawer.

EFFECT OF SMOKE

Once overpowered by smoke, bees lose all combative propensities, their anger turning to submission. However, after the effects of the smoke have passed, their animosity will return.

Should any resentment be shown on raising a hive, blow in the smoke and they immediately retreat, "begging pardon." After a few times, they learn "it's no use," and allow an inspection. If you wish to take off a box, raise it just enough to blow under the smoke; there is no trouble; you can replace it with another; the bees are kept out of the way with a little more smoke, *and no anger about it will be remembered.*

Those in the box are all submission; they can be carried away and handled as you please, without a possibility of getting them irritated, until they once more get home, and then are much more "amiable" than if the box had been taken without the smoke.

In short, by using smoke on occasions where the bees would be disturbed by our meddling, their combative propensities are kept dormant.

Those who are accustomed to smoking will find a pipe or cigar very convenient here.

REMEDIES FOR THE STING OF A BEE

Concerning the remedies for stings, it is difficult to tell which is the best. There is so much difference in the effect on different individuals, and different parts of the body, as well as the depth of the sting, that there are a variety of remedies to consider.

These remedies include saleratus and water, salt and water, soft-soap mixed with salt, a raw onion cut in two and one-half applied, mud or clay mixed pretty wet and changed often, tobacco wet and rubbed thoroughly to get at the strength, and cold water constantly applied. To cure the smart, the application of tobacco is strongly urged, and cold water helps prevent the swelling.

The first thing to be done after being stung is to pull the stinger out of the wound as quickly as possible. Even after it is torn from the bee, the muscles that control it continue to operate and it penetrates deeper and deeper into the flesh, injecting more of its poison into the wound.

Every apiarian should keep close at hand a small magnifying glass, so that he can without delay find and remove a stinger. In most cases if removed it will avoid serious consequences; whereas if left it may cause inflammation and suffering.

After the stinger is removed, care should be taken not to irritate the wound by rubbing. No matter how intense the smarting, applying friction to the wound should be avoided as the poison will be carried through the circulation system and severe consequences may ensue.

As most of the popular remedies are rubbed in, they can compound the problem. Be careful not to *suck* the wound as many are inclined to do for this produces irritation in the same way as rubbing.

If the mouth is applied to the wound, other unpleasant consequences may occur. The poison of the bee acts not only on the circulation system but also on certain organs. Distressing headaches are often the result.

From my own experience, I recommend *cold water* as the best remedy for the sting of a bee. This may be applied by wetting a cloth and holding it gently to the wound. Cold water acts in two ways: Being very volatile, the poison of the bee is quickly dissolved in water; and the coldness of the water has a tendency to check inflammation and prevent the virus from being absorbed into the system.

The leaves of the plantain, crushed and applied to the wound, will prove a good substitute when water is not easily available.

Some recommend the use of spirits of hartshorn, applied directly to the wound.

The immediate extraction of the stinger, even if nothing more is done, proves to be much more efficacious than any remedy that can be applied. Not removing the stinger allows it discharge all its venom into the wound.

It may be some comfort to know that after a while the bee's poison will produce less and less effect upon your system. When I first became interested in bees, a sting was quite a formidable thing, the pain often very intense, with the wound sometimes swelling as to obstruct my sight. At present, after many stings over the years, the pain is slight, and if I can quickly extract the stinger, no unpleasant consequences ensue, even when no remedies are used.

There's a highly amusing remedy propounded by an old English apiarian. He advises that the person who has been stung should catch another bee and make it sting on the same spot! To try this unusual homeopathic remedy, I allowed a bee to sting me on the finger, then allowed another bee to insert its stinger as near as possible in the same spot. I used no remedies of any kind. Thanks to my zeal for new discoveries, I suffered more pain and swelling than I'd experienced in years.

So beware of apocryphal advice.

Basics of ... Beekeeping

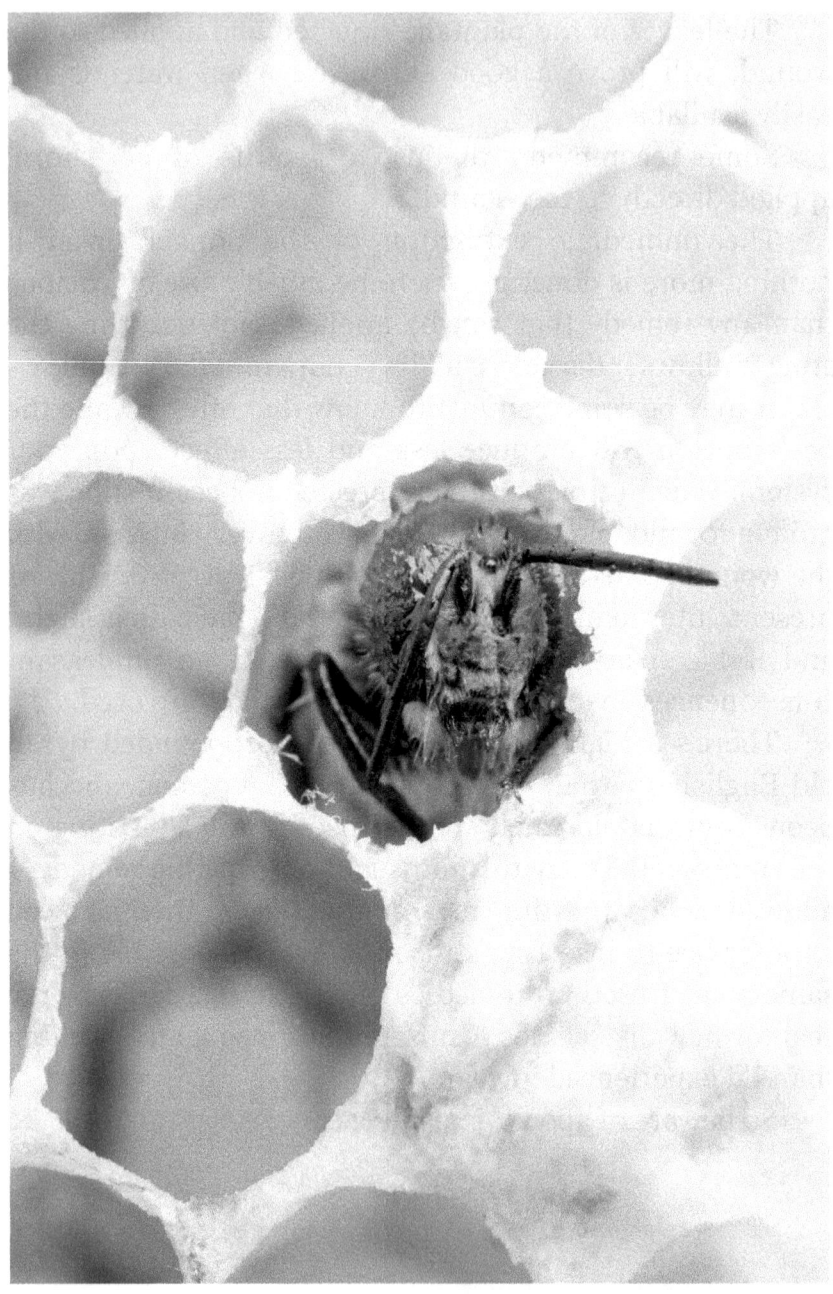

CHAPTER EIGHT

BREEDING

The period at which bees commence depositing eggs depends on the strength of the colony, amount of honey on hand, etc., and not the time they start gathering food.

When the Queen is about to lay, she puts her head into a cell and remains in that position for a second or two to ascertain its fitness for the deposit she's about to make. She then withdraws her head and curving her body downwards inserts the lower part of it into the cell: in a few seconds she turns half round upon herself and withdraws, leaving an egg behind her. She lays a considerable number of eggs, equally on each side of the comb, those on the one side being exactly opposite to those on the other as far as the relative position of the cells will admit. This is to produce the utmost concentration and economy of heat for developing the various changes of the brood.

HOW SMALL STOCKS COMMENCE

The first eggs are deposited in the center of the cluster of bees, in a small family. It may not be in the center of the hive in *all* cases; but the middle of the cluster is the warmest place.

Here the Queen will first commence. A few cells, or a space not larger than a dollar, are first used, those exactly opposite on the same comb are next occupied. If the warmth of the hive will allow, whether mild weather produces it, or the family be large enough to generate that which is artificial, appears to make no difference; she will then take the next combs exactly corresponding with the first commencement but not quite as large a place is used as in the first comb.

The circle of eggs in the first is then enlarged, and more are added in the next, etc., continuing to spread to the next combs, keeping the distance to the outside of the circle of eggs, to the center or place of beginning, about equal on all sides, until they occupy the outside comb. Long before the outside comb is occupied, the first eggs deposited are matured, and the Queen will return to the center, and use these cells again, but is not so particular this time to fill so many in such exact order as at first. This is the general process of small or medium sized families. I have removed the bees from such, in all stages of breeding, and always found their proceedings as described.

DIFFERENT WITH LARGER ONES

But with very large families, their proceedings are different: as any part of the cluster of bees is warm enough for breeding, there is less necessity for economizing heat, and having all the eggs confined to one small spot, some unoccupied cells will be found among the brood; a few will contain honey and beebread.

HOW POLLEN IS STORED IN THE BREEDING SEASON

In the height of the breeding season, a circle of cells nearly all beebread, an inch or two wide, will border the sheets of comb containing brood. As beebread is probably the principal food of the young bee, it is thus very convenient.

When pollen is abundant, they soon reach the outside sheets of comb with the brood.

Before depositing an egg, the Queen enters the cell head first, probably to ascertain if it is in proper condition to receive it. Thus, a cell part filled with beebread or honey is never used. If the area of combs is small, or the family is small, and cannot protect a large space with the necessary heat, she will often deposit two, and sometimes three, in one cell. But under prosperous circumstances, with a hive of suitable size, etc., this emergency is avoided.

OPERATION OF LAYING AND THE EGGS DESCRIBED

When a cell is found in condition to receive the egg, the Queen on withdrawing her head immediately curves her abdomen and inserts it into the cell for a few seconds. Afterwards, an egg will be found attached by one end to the bottom. The egg is about the sixteenth of an inch in length, slightly curved, very small, nearly uniform the whole length, abruptly rounded at the ends, semi-transparent, and covered with a very thin and extremely delicate coat, often breaking with the slightest touch.

After the egg has been in the cell about three days, a small white worm -- the larva -- is seen coiled in the bottom.

TIME FROM THE EGG TO THE PERFECT BEE

In about six days the cell is sealed over with a convex waxen lid. The larva is now hidden from sight for about twelve days, until it bites off the cover and emerges as a perfect bee.

The period from the egg to the perfect bee varies from twenty to twenty-four days, the average being about twenty-two for Workers, twenty-four for Drones.

TERMS FOR YOUNG BEES

The young bee, when it first leaves the egg, is termed grub, maggot, worm, or larva; from this state it changes to the shape of the perfect bee, which is said to be three days after finishing the cocoon.

From the time of this change, till it is ready to leave the cell, the terms nymph, pupa, and chrysalis, are applied.

COMING OUT

The lid of the Drone's cell is rather more convex than that of the Worker's, and when removed by the young bee to work its way out, is left nearly perfect. Being cut off around the edges, a good coat or lining of silk keeps it whole. The covering of the Worker's cell is mostly wax, and is pretty well cut to pieces by the time the bee gets out. The covering to the Queen's cell is like the Drone's, but larger in diameter, and thicker, being lined with a little more silk.

ROUGH TREATMENT OF THE YOUNG BEE

Instead of care or notice, these young bees often receive rather rough treatment: the Workers sometimes come in contact with one part way out the cell, with force sufficient to almost dislocate its neck; yet they do not stop to see if any harm is done, or beg pardon. The little sufferer, after this rude lesson, scrambles back as soon as possible out of the way; enlarges the prison door a little, and attempts again, with perhaps the same success: a dozen trials are often made before they succeed. When it does actually leave, it seems like a stranger in a multitude, with no friend to counsel, or mother to direct. It wanders about uncared for and unheeded, and rarely finds one sufficiently benevolent to bestow even the necessaries of life; but does sometimes. It is *generally* forced to learn the important lesson of looking out for itself the day it leaves the cradle. A cell containing honey is sought for, where its immediate wants are all supplied.

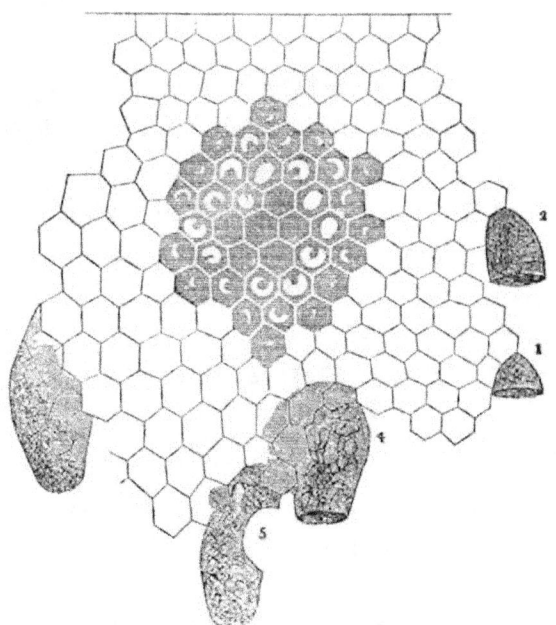

THE THREE KINDS OF CELLS

The preceding plate represents a piece of comb containing all the different cells – those at the left hand the size for Drones. In the center are few that appear sealed over, others nearly covered, others the larva in different stages of growth, as well as the eggs. *Fig. 1* represents a Queen's cell just commenced. They are usually started thus far the first season, very frequently when the hive is only half or two-thirds full. *Fig. 2* is a cell sufficiently advanced to receive the egg. *Fig. 3* one finished, the stage when the first swarm leaves. *Fig. 4* when a Queen has been perfected and left. *Fig. 5* is a cell where its occupant has been destroyed by a rival, and removed by the Workers. It will be perceived that each finished Queen's cell contains as much wax as fifty made for the Workers.

A TEST FOR THE PRESENCE OF A QUEEN

If you have a hive that you suspect has lost a Queen, her presence can be ascertained by this method: Sweep the board clean, and look the next day or two for eggs. When one or more egg is found, no further proof of the presence of a Queen is needed.

WHEN DRONES ARE REARED

Whenever the hive is well supplied with honey, and plenty of bees, a portion of eggs are deposited in the Drone cells, which three or four days more are necessary to mature than the Worker.

WHEN QUEENS ARE REARED

When the combs become crowded with bees, and honey plenty, the preparations for young Queens commence: as the first step towards swarming, from one to twenty royal cells are begun; when about half completed, the Queen (if all continues favorable) will deposit eggs in them, these will be glued fast by one end like those for the Workers; there is no doubt but they are precisely the same kind of eggs that produce other bees. When hatched, the little worm will be supplied with a superabundance of food; at least, it appears so from the fact that a few times I have found a quantity remaining in the cell after the Queen had left. The consistence of this food is about like cream, the color some lighter, or just tinged with yellow. If it was thin like water, or even honey, I cannot imagine how it could be made to stay in the upper end of an inverted cell of that size in such quantities as are put in, as the bees often fill it near half full. Sometimes a cell of this kind will contain this food, and no worm to feed upon it. I *guessed* the bees had compounded more than their present necessities required, and that they stored it there to have it ready, also, that being there all might know it was for royalty.

LIABILITY OF BEING DESTROYED

In any stage from egg to maturity these royal insects are liable to be destroyed – if honey fails from any cause sufficient to make the existence of a swarm any way hazardous, the preparations are abandoned, and these young Queens destroyed.

DRONES DESTROYED

When an occurrence like the above happens, the Drones next fall victims to the failure of honey. A brief existence only is theirs; such as are perfect, are destroyed without mercy; those in the chrysalis state are often dragged out, and sacrificed to the necessities of the family. Such as are allowed to hatch, instead of being fed and protected as they would be if honey was abundant, are allowed, while yet weak from the effects of hunger, to wander from the hive, and fall to the earth by hundreds. These effects attend only a scarcity in the early part of the season. The massacre of July and September is quite different.

The Drones then have age and strength – an effort is apparently first made by the Workers to drive them out without proceeding to extremes; they are harassed sometimes for several days; the Workers feigning only to sting, or else they cannot, as I never succeeded in seeing but very few dispatched in that way; yet there is evidence proving beyond doubt that the sting is used.

Hundreds will often be collected together in a compact body at the bottom of the hive; this mutual protection affording a few hours' respite from their tormentors, who do not cease to worry them.

In a few days they are gone, and it is a hard matter to tell what has become of them, at least the majority. If the hive in September is well supplied with honey, a portion of the Drones has a longer lease of life given them; I have seen them as late as December.

In some seasons, when the best hives are poorly supplied with stores, the ensuing spring the bees will rear no Drones, until the flowers yield a good supply. I have known one or two years in which no Drones appeared before the last of June; at other times, thousands are matured by the first of May.

OLD QUEEN LEAVES WITH FIRST SWARM

The old Queen leaves with the first swarm; as soon as cells are ready in the new hive she will deposit her eggs in them, at first for Workers; the number perfected will correspond with the supply of honey and size of the swarm. When the supply fails before leaving the old stock, she remains *there*, and continues laying throughout the season; but the bees matured after the 20th of July (in this section) are not more than sufficient to keep the number good. As many die, or are lost during their excursions, as the young ones will replace; in fact, they often lose rather than gain; so that by the next spring, a hive that has cast no swarm, is no better for a stock than one from which a swarm has issued. We are apt to be deceived by bees clustering outside, towards the latter end of the season, and suppose it hardly possible for them all to get in, when it may be caused by hot weather, full stores, etc.

A YOUNG QUEEN REPLACES HER MOTHER IN THE OLD STOCK

In ordinary circumstances, when a swarm has left a stock, the oldest of the young Queens is ready to emerge from her cell in about eight or nine days; if no second swarm is sent out, she will take her mother's place, and begin to lay eggs in about ten days, or a little less. Two or three weeks is the only time throughout the whole season, but what eggs can be found in all prosperous hives. Whenever a copious yield of honey occurs, Drones are reared; as it becomes scarce, they are destroyed.

The relative number of Drones and Workers that exist when they are most numerous, doubtless depends on the size of the hive, whether one in ten, or one in thirty.

When a swarm is first hived, the first cells are the size for working; if the hive be very small, and bees numerous, it may be filled before they are fully aware of it, and but few Drone-cells constructed; consequently, but few can be raised; whereas if the hive be large, long before it is full, considerable honey will be stored. Cells for storing honey are usually the size for Drones; these will be made as soon as the requisite number for Workers is provided. An abundant yield of honey during the process of filling a large hive, would therefore cause a great proportion of these cells to be built – the amount of Drone-brood being governed by the same cause, is a strong argument against large hives, as affording room for too many of these cells, where an unnecessary number of Drones will be reared, causing a useless expenditure of honey, etc.

Basics of ... Beekeeping

CHAPTER NINE

BEE PASTURAGE

In some seasons the earth is covered with snow much later than others. When this occurs, a greater number of warm days are necessary to melt it and start the flowers than otherwise.

THREE PRINCIPAL SOURCES OF HONEY

There are three principal sources of honey, viz.: – clover, basswood, and buckwheat. But clover is the only one of universal dependence; as that is found almost everywhere in the country. Buckwheat in some places is the main source; in others, basswood, which is of brief duration.

Where all three are abundant, there is the true El Dorado of the apiarian! With plenty of clover and buckwheat, it is nearly as well. Even with clover alone, enormous quantities of honey are obtained.

PASTURAGE

Willows are among the most desirable trees to have within reach of the bees: some kinds of willow put out their catkins very early, and yield an abundance of beebread and nectar. All the willows furnish an abundance of food for the bees; and as there is considerable difference in the time of their blossoming, it is desirable to have such varieties as will furnish the bees with food, as long as possible.

The Sugar Maple furnishes a large supply of very delicious honey, and its blossoms hanging in drooping fringes, will be all alive with bees.

The Apricot, Peach, Plum and Cherry are much frequented by the bees.

Pears and Apples furnish copious supplies of honey.

The Tulip tree (*Liriodendron*) is probably one of the greatest honey-producing trees in the world. In rich lands this magnificent tree will grow over one hundred feet high, and when covered with its large bell-shaped blossoms of mingled green and golden yellow, it is one of the most beautiful trees in the world. The blossoms are expanding in succession, often for more than two weeks, and a new swarm will frequently fill its hive from these trees alone. The honey though dark in color, possesses a rich flavor. This tree has been successfully cultivated as a shade tree.

The American Linden, or Bass Wood, is another tree that yields large supplies of white honey. It is one of our most beautiful native trees, and ought to be planted much more extensively than it is, in our villages and countryseats. The Linden blossoms soon after the white clover begins to fail, and a majestic tree covered with its yellow clusters, at a season when very few blossoms are to be seen, is a sight most beautiful and refreshing.

However, the English Linden is worthless for bees, and in many places, has been so infested by worms, as to make it necessary to cut it down.

WHITE CLOVER

Of all the various sources from which the bees derive their supplies, white clover is the most important. It yields large quantities of very white honey, of the purest quality, and wherever it flourishes in abundance, the honeybee will always gather a rich harvest. In this country at least, it seems to be the most certain reliance of the apiary. It blossoms at a season of the year when the weather is usually both dry and hot, and the bees gather the honey from it, after the sun has dried off the dew: so that its juices are very thick, and almost ready to be sealed over at once in the cells.

Sweet-scented clover (*Mellilotus Leucantha,*) affords a rich bee-pasturage. It blossoms the second year from the seed, and grows to a great height, and is always swarming with bees until quite late in the fall. Attempts have been made to cultivate it for the sake of its value as a hay crop, but it has been found too coarse in its texture, to be very profitable. Where many bees are kept, it might however, be so valuable for them as to justify its extensive cultivation. During the early part of the season, it might be mowed and fed to the cattle, in a green and tender state, and allowed to blossom later in the season, when the bees can find but few sources to gather from.

ADVANTAGES OF BUCKWHEAT

Between the 20th of July and the 10th of August, buckwheat flowers provide a second harvest. In many places it's bees' main source for surplus honey. Many consider it an inferior quality. The color, when separated from comb, resembles molasses. The taste is more pungent than clover honey; it is prized on that account by some, and disliked by others for the same reason.

Buckwheat comes at a season when it is highly

important to the bees, and they are often able to fill their hives with a generous supply against winter.

ALDER

The first material gathered from flowers is pollen. Candle-alder (*Alnus Rubra*) yields the first supply. The time of flowering varies from the 10th of March to the 20th of April. The amount afforded is also variable. Cold, freezing weather frequently destroys a great portion of these flowers after they are out.

These staminate flowers are nearly perfected the season previous, and a few warm days in spring will bring them out, even before any leaves appear. When the weather continues fine, great quantities of farina are secured.

The time that bees commence their labors does not govern the time of swarming; that depends on the weather through April and May.

Our swamps produce several varieties of willow (*Salix*) that put out their blossoms very irregularly. Some of these bushes are a month earlier than others, and some of the buds on the same bush are a week or two later than the rest. These also afford only pollen, but are much more dependence than alder, as a turn of cold weather cannot at any time destroy more than a small part. Next comes the aspen, (*Populus Tremuloides*). Of this we have more than necessary for any purpose. It is not a particular favorite with the bees, as but few, comparatively, visit it.

It is followed very soon by an abundance of the red maple (*Acer Rubrum*), that suits them better, but this, like the others, is often lost by freezing.

The first honey obtained of any account is from the golden willow (*Salix Vitellina*); it yields no pollen, and is seldom injured by frost.

Gooseberries, currants, cherries, pear and peach trees, add a share of both honey and pollen. Sugar maple (*Acer Saccharinum*) now throws out its ten thousand silken tassels, beautiful as gold. Strawberries modestly open their petals in invitation, but, like "obscure virtues," are often neglected for the more conspicuous Dandelion, and the showy appearance and flagrant blossoms of the apple-trees, which now open their stores, offering to their acceptance a real harvest.

RED RASPBERRY A FAVORITE

The red raspberry (*Rubus Strigosus*) next presents the stamens as the most conspicuous part of the flower, soliciting the embrace of the bee by pouring out bounteous libations more prized by our industrious insect than wine. For several weeks they are allowed to partake of this exquisite beverage.

CATNIP, MOTHERWORT, AND HOARHOUND

Catnip (*Nepeta Cataria*), Motherwort (*Leonurus Cardiaca*), and Horehound (*Marrubium Vulgare*) put forth their flowers about the middle of June. Rich in sweetness, the bees visit them at all hours and in nearly all kinds of weather. They last from four to six weeks; the catnip even longer.

The flower of the Ox-eye daisy (*Leucanthemum Vulgare*) is compound, with each little floret containing particles so minute that the task of obtaining a load is very tedious. It is only visited when other flowers are scarce.

Snapdragon (*Linaria Vulgaris*), with its nauseous odor, is made to bestow the only good thing about it, except its beauty, upon our insect. The flower is large and tubular, and the bee must enter it; but soon emerges covered with dust. This is not brushed into pellets on its legs, like the pollen from other flowers, but adheres to its back between the wings, remaining there sometimes for months.

Bush honey-suckle (*Diervilla Trifida*) is popular.

Also Mustard (*Sinapis Nigra*) is a great favorite.

I have now mentioned most of the honey-producing trees and plants that come on before the middle of July. The course of these flowers is termed the first yield.

FRUIT FLOWERS IMPORTANT IN GOOD WEATHER

In good weather, during this period of apple blossoms, a gain of twenty pounds is sometimes added to the bees' stores.

However, a frost at this time can destroy all, with the gain of our bees being reversed, lighter at the end than at the beginning of these flowers.

If good weather, we can expect our first swarms about the first of June; if not, no subsequent yield of honey will make up for this deficiency. We now have a time of several days, from ten to fourteen, in which but few flowers exist. If hives are poorly supplied when this scarcity occurs, it will so disarrange the bees' plans for swarming that no preparations are made again before July, and sometimes not at all.

In regions where the wild cherry (*Cerasus Seratina*) abounds, those flowers will fill this time of scarcity for our bees.

GARDEN FLOWERS UNIMPORTANT

I have not mentioned garden flowers, because the amount obtained from them is small compared to the forest and fields. It is especially true of ornamental flowers like Hollyhock (*Altha Rosea*) and Mallows (*Malva Rotundifolia*).

A person expecting his hives to be filled from such a source would be very disappointed.

WHAT SEASON IS BEST FOR HONEY?

The inquiry is often made, "What kind of season is best for bees, wet or dry?" This point I have watched very closely, and have found that a medium between the two extremes produces most honey.

When farmers begin to express fears of a drought, then is the time (if in the season of flowers) that most honey is obtained; but if dry weather passes these limits, the quantity is greatly diminished. Of the two extremes, perhaps very wet is the worst.

HOW MANY STOCKS SHOULD BE KEPT

"What number of stocks can there be kept in one place?" is another question often asked. This is like Mr. A. asking farmer B. how many cattle could be pastured in a lot of ten acres.

Farmer B. would first wish to know how much pasture said lot would produce, before he could begin to answer;

Basics of ... Beekeeping

since one lot of that size might produce ten times as much as the other. So with bees, one apiary of two hundred stocks might find honey in abundance for all, and another of forty might almost starve. Like the cattle, it depends on pasture.

Basics of ... Beekeeping

CHAPTER TEN

BEESWAX

Wax is a natural secretion of the bees; it may be called their oil or fat. Mainly it consists of esters of fatty acids and various long-chain alcohols.

This wax is formed by worker bees, which secrete it from eight wax-producing mirror glands on the inner sides of the sternites (the ventral shield or plate of each segment of the body) on abdominal segments 4 to 7.

If the bees are gorged with honey, or any liquid sweet, and remain quietly clustered together, it comes out in the shape of very delicate scales. Soon after a swarm is hived, the bottom board will be covered with these scales.

Honeybees use this beeswax to build honeycomb cells in which their young are raised.

BUILDING COMBS

When a swarm of bees is leaving the parent stock, three-fourths or more of them will fill their sacks with honey. A large swarm will carry with them some five or six pounds of honey from the parent stock. Perhaps eight pounds, for large swarms.

When located in their new home, of course no cells exist to hold it, so it must remain in the sack for several hours.

Thin white scales of wax, about a sixteenth of an inch in diameter, somewhat circular, are formed between the rings of the abdomen. With the claws of one of their hind legs, one of these is detached and conveyed to the mouth, and there pinched with their forceps or teeth, until one edge is worked somewhat rough. It is then applied to the comb being constructed, or to the roof of the hive. The first rudiments of comb are often applied within the first half hour after the swarm is hived.

Whenever the bees have more honey than the combs will hold, if there is room in the hive, they will construct more combs. They have a compulsion to fill the hive.

Drone-cells are seldom made in the top of the hive, but a part are generally joined on the Worker-cells, a little distance from the top; others near the bottom. There seems to be no rule about the number of such cells. Some hives will contain twice the number of others. It may depend on the yield of honey at the time; when very plenty, more Drone cells, etc. If the hive be very large, no doubt an unprofitable number would be constructed. Where the large and small cells join, there will be some cells of irregular shape; some with four or five angles; the distance from one angle to the other is also varied. Even where two combs of cells the same size join, making a straight comb, they are not always perfect.

MANNER OF WORKING WAX

Transferring the swarms to different hives from one to forty-eight hours after being hived will show their progress. I have found that wax is attached to the top of the hive at first promiscuously, that is, without the least order, until some of the blocks or lumps are sufficiently advanced for them to begin cells. The scales of wax are welded on the edge quite thick, without regard to the shape of the cell, then an excavation is made on one side for the bottom of a cell, and two others on the opposite side; the division between them exactly opposite the center of the first. When this piece is an inch or two in length, two other pieces at equal distances on each side are commenced.

If the swarm is large, and honey abundant, it is common for two pieces of comb to be started at one time on different parts of the top; the sheets in the two places are often at right angles, or any other way, just as chance happens to give direction. The little lumps that are placed at random at first are all removed as they advance.

While the combs are in progress, the edges are always kept much the thickest, and the base of the cell is worked down to the proper thickness with their teeth, and polished smooth as glass. The ends of the cell also, as they lengthen them, will always be found much thicker than any other part of it when finished.

When two combs approach each other in the middle of the hive at nearly right angles, an edge of comb is left there; but when an obtuse angle, the edges are generally joined, making a sheet of crooked comb. It is evident where the two combs join, there must be some irregular cells unfit for rearing brood.

SOME WAX WASTED

When constructing comb, they are constantly wasting wax, either accidentally or voluntarily. The next morning after a swarm is located, the scales may be found, and will continue to increase as long as they are working it; the quantity often amounts to a handful or more.

The angles in the cells used for brood, are gradually

filled, and after a time become round, both at the ends and sides.

WATER NECESSARY TO COMB-MAKING

Whenever bees are engaged making comb, a supply of water is absolutely necessary.

June, and first part of July, and most part of August (the season of buckwheat,) are periods of extensive comb-making; they then use most water; breeding is carried on from March till October, and as extensively in May, perhaps more so, than in August, yet not a tenth part of the water is used in May.

As they get sufficient honey to require more comb to store it, they will at the same time have a brood; and it is easy to guess they need it for brood as comb.

When no pond, brook, spring, or other source is within convenient distance, the apiarian would find it economy to place some within their reach, as it would save much valuable time, if they would otherwise have to go a great distance, when they might be more profitably employed. It should be situated so that the bees can obtain it without jeopardizing their lives – a barrel or pail has sides so steep that many will slip off and drown. A trough made very shallow, with a good broad strip around the edge to afford an alighting place, should be provided. The middle should contain a float, or a handful of shavings spread in the water with a few small stones laid on them to prevent their being blown away when the water is out, is very convenient.

A tin dish an inch or so in depth, will do very well. The quantity needed may be ascertained by what is used – only give them enough, and change it daily.

I have no trouble of this kind, as there is a stream of water within a few yards of the hives; but I have an opportunity to witness something of the number engaged in carrying it. Thousands may be seen (in June and August) filling their sacks, while a continual stream is on the wing, going and returning.

Basics of ... Beekeeping

CHAPTER ELEVEN

PROPOLIS

Propolis is a red or brown resinous substance collected by honeybees from tree buds. It is used by them to fill crevices and to seal and varnish honeycombs. Think of it as "bee glue."

A mixture of wax and propolis is used by the bees to strengthen the attachments of the combs to the top and sides of the hive, and serves most admirably for this purpose, as it is much more adhesive than wax alone. If the combs, as soon as they are built, are not filled with honey or brood, they are beautifully varnished with a most delicate coating of this material, which adds exceedingly to their strength: but as this natural varnish impairs their delicate whiteness, they ought not to be allowed to remain in the surplus honey receptacles, accessible to the bees, unless when they are actively engaged in storing them with honey.

The bees make a very liberal use of this substance to fill up all the crevices about their premises: and as the natural summer heat of the hive keeps it soft, the bee moth selects it as a proper place of deposit for her eggs. For this reason, the hive should be made of sound lumber, entirely free from cracks, and thoroughly painted on the inside as well as outside.

PLASTERING

The first swarms that issue in May, or early June, seldom use much of the article for soldering and plastering; but instead a composition the most of which is wax. As a result, when old pieces of boards that had been used for hives, were left in the sun, that this old propolis would become soft in the middle of the day.

Bees frequently are observed packing propolis upon their legs. It was detached in small particles. The bee does not fly during this operation, as it does while packing pollen.

Cracks, large enough for bees to pass through, are sometimes completely filled with it. In this season, a little before sunset of some fair day, I have frequently seen the bees enter the hive with what I supposed to be the pure article on their legs, like pollen, except the surface, which would be smooth and glossy; the color much lighter than when it gets age.

When a bee requires a little, it seizes hold of the pellet with its teeth or forceps, and detaches a portion. The whole lump will not cleave off at once; but firmly adheres to the leg; from its tenacity, perhaps a string an inch long will be formed in separating, the piece obtained is immediately applied to their work, and the bee is ready to supply another with a portion; it doubtless gets rid of its load in this way.

Basics of ... Beekeeping

CHAPTER TWELVE

FEEDING

Feeding bees in spring is sometimes necessary. Occasionally stocks consume more honey than expected, or are robbed, so offering a little care may save a loss.

Bees at this season of the year consume a very large quantity of honey: they are stimulated to great activity by the returning warmth, and are therefore compelled to eat much more than when they were almost dormant among their combs.

In addition to this extra demand, they are now engaged in rearing thousands of young, and all these require a liberal supply of food.

If the beekeeper ascertains that his bees do not have sufficient food, he must at once supply them with what they need.

It is wrong to begin to feed without being prepared to continue to do so, as the supply must be kept up till honey is abundant.

BAD BEEKEEPING

What farmer would neglect the wants of his cattle, and allow them to drop down lifeless in their stalls, or in his barnyard, when the fields in a few weeks will be green with the mantle of spring?

Yet, thousands of bee swarms perish annually owing to neglect. Let such an apiarist be ashamed that he refused to feed his bees the few pounds of sugar or honey which would have saved their lives ... and enabled them to repay him tenfold for his care.

EARLY FEEDING

By judicious early feeding, a whole apiary may be not only encouraged to breed much faster than they would have done otherwise, but they will increase their stores with unusual rapidity.

And as soon as they begin to gather pollen from the fields, this feeding should be discontinued.

CARE NEEDED

Honey fed to bees is almost certain to cause quarrels among them. Sometimes strong stocks scent the honey given to weak ones, and carry it off as fast as supplied.

Also caution must be exercised to prevent your bees from filling up the cells that ought to be used for the brood with this proffered honey. To be sure, bees will take all that they can and stow it in their cells. However, the result of filling up brood combs with honey instead of eggs is that the hive's future population may become reduced in numbers! Thus, the inexperienced apiarian has made a situation worse.

HOW LONG TO WAIT BEFORE FEEDING

If it is wished to wait as long as possible, and not lose the bees, a test will be necessary to decide how long it will do to delay feeding.

In this case, *they will need examination every morning.* If a light tap on the hive is answered by a brisk, lively buzzing, they are not suffering yet. But if no answer is returned, it indicates a want of strength.

Some bees may be too weak to remain among the combs, and can be found lying on the bottom, and some few outside. If the weather is cool, they appear to be lifeless; yet they can be revived, and now *must he fed*.

DIRECTIONS FOR FEEDING

Those among the combs may be able to move, though feebly. When this is the case, invert the hive, gather up all the scattered bees, and put them in.

Get some honey. If candied, heat it till it dissolves. Comb honey is not so good without mashing it up. And if no honey is on hand, brown sugar may be used instead.

Add a little water, and boil it till about the consistence of honey, and skim it; when cool enough, pour a quantity among the combs, directly on the bees. Cover the bottom of the hive with a cloth, securing it firmly, and bring to the fire to warm up. In two or three hours they will be revived, and may be returned to the stand, providing the honey given is all taken up.

The necessity of a daily visit to the hives is required, because if left for one day in the situation just described, it will be too late to revive them.

At night, if you have a box cover, such as I have recommended, you may open the holes in the top of the hive; fill a small baking dish with honey or syrup, and set it on the top; put in some shavings to keep the bees from drowning, or a float may be used if you choose; it should be made of some very light wood, very thin, and full of holes or narrow channels, made with a saw.

At the commencement of feeding, a few drops should

be scattered on the top of the hive and trailed to the side of the dish, to teach them the way. After feeding a few times, they will know the route.

If the family is very small, what honey is left in the morning may attract other bees, so keep a good lookout that they are not plundered, and left again in a starving condition, until flowers produce sufficient food.

WHOLE FAMILIES MAY DESERT THE HIVE

When you have the means to keep up a supply of food, and time requisite to make feeding secure, perhaps it would not be advisable to wait till the last extremity before feeding, as a small family will sometimes entirely desert the hive, when destitute, if it occurs before they have much brood. In these cases, they issue as a swarm. After flying a long time, they either return, or unite with some other stock.

If they return, they need attention immediately. You may be certain there is something wrong, let the desertion take place when it may; in spring it may be destitution, or moldy combs; at other times the presence of worms, diseased brood, etc. By whatever the cause, ascertain it and apply a remedy.

FEEDING TO INDUCE EARLY SWARMS

If the object in feeding is to induce early swarms, the best stocks should be chosen for the purpose. One pound per day is enough, perhaps too much. Begin feeding the bees as soon as you can make them take it up in spring, and continue until white clover blossoms, or swarms issue.

Another object in feeding bees at this period is to have

the store combs all filled with inferior honey, so that when clover blossoms appear (which yields the best honey) there is no room for the bees to store it except in the boxes.

Basics of ... Beekeeping

CHAPTER THIRTEEN
PUTTING ON AND TAKING OFF BOXES

Today, most beehives are based on the Langstroth design: stacked boxes with moveable frames. The advantage of this hive is that the bees build honeycomb into frames, which can be removed with ease. The boxes allow stock to be swapped, swarms to be collected, and additional storage for honey created.

Putting on boxes comes between spring and summer. No need to do this before the first of May, because it is generally useless if the hive isn't full of bees. You don't want to allow any animal heat to escape, for warmth is needed in the hive to mature the brood.

WHEN TO PUT ON BOXES

Some experience is necessary to know the best time boxes are needed. Generally speaking, when bees begin to obtain honey is the time to put on the boxes. Put on only one at first; when this is full of honey and bees are crowded outside, another box can be added. The object of putting on boxes before swarming is to employ those bees that otherwise would remain idle, clustering outside while preparing the young Queens for swarming. But more room is unnecessary to engage these bees profitably in producing addition honey for the hive.

FILLING A BOX

It usually takes three or four weeks to fill a box. Two

weeks is the shortest time I've ever experienced. This timing, of course, depends on the yield of honey and size of the swarm.

WHEN TO TAKE OFF BOXES PART FULL

When no more honey is being added, all boxes that are worth the trouble should be taken off. If left longer, the comb gets darker. And the bees generally will move any cells of honey not sealed over down into the hive.

TOBACCO SMOKE PREFERRED TO SLIDES

When boxes are taken off, using a slide of tin, etc., to close the holes, some of the bees are apt to be crushed, and others may find themselves minus a head, leg, or abdomen. You can expect the colony to be irritable for several days.

A little tobacco smoke will keep them quiet. Just raise the box to be taken off sufficiently to puff some smoke under it, and the bees will leave the vicinity of the holes in an instant. Thus, the box can then be removed – and another put on if necessary – without exciting their anger in the least.

MANNER OF DISPOSING OF THE BEES IN THE BOXES

Arouse the bees by striking the box lightly four or five times. If all the cells are finished, and honey is still obtained, turn the box bottom up, near the hive from which it was taken, so that the bees can enter it without flying. By this means you can save several young bees that have never left the hive.

Boxes can be taken off either in the morning or

evening. If in the morning, it can stand several hours when the sun is not too hot, but on no account leave it standing in the sun in the middle of the day as the combs will melt.

BEES DISPOSED TO CARRY AWAY HONEY

When boxes are taken off at the end of the honey season, a different method of getting rid of the bees must be adopted, or you will lose your honey. (We will lose some anyway, as most of the bees fill themselves before leaving; they will carry it home and return for more, if not prevented.)

When a large number of boxes are to be managed, a more expeditious mode is to have a large box with close joints, or an empty hogshead, or a few barrels with one head out, set in some convenient place; put the boxes in, one above another, but not in a manner to stop the holes; over the top throw a thin sheet. The bees will leave the boxes, creep to the top, and get on the sheet; take this off and turn it over a few times, in this way getting rid of them without the possibility of carrying off much honey. All that know the way will return to the hive, but a few young ones are lost.

NOT DISPOSED TO STING

They seldom offer to sting during this part of the operation, even when the box is taken off without tobacco smoke, and carried away from the hive; after a little time, the bees finding themselves away from home, lose all animosity.

As honey becomes scarce, less brood is reared; a great many cells that they occupied are soon empty; also, several cells that contained honey have been drained, and used to mature the portion of brood just started at the time of the failure. We can now understand, or think we do, why our best stocks that are very heavy, that but a few days before were crowded for room and storing in boxes, are now eager for honey to store in the hive; as there is abundant room for several pounds. They will quickly remove to the hive the contents of any box left exposed; or even risk their lives by entering a neighboring hive for it; after being allowed to make a beginning, under such circumstances.

RULE

During a yield of honey, take off boxes as fast as they are filled, and put on empty ones. At the end of the season take all off. Not one stock in a hundred will starve that has worked in boxes, that is, when the hive is the proper size, and full before adding the boxes, unless robbed or other casualty.

Basics of ... Beekeeping

CHAPTER FOURTEEN

SWARMING

The season for regular swarms commences around the middle of May. The end is about the 15th of the latter month, with some exceptions.

The subject now before us is one of thrilling interest. To the apiarian the prospect of an increase of stocks is sufficient to create some interest, even when the phenomenon of swarming would fail to awaken it. But to the naturalist this season has charms that the indifferent beholder can never realize.

MEANS OF UNDERSTANDING IT

It's important for an apiarian to understand the *modus operandi* of swarming.

Regular swarms take place something like this: Before they commence, two or three things are requisite. The combs must be crowded with bees; they must contain a numerous brood advancing from the egg to maturity; the bees must be obtaining honey either by being fed or from flowers. Being crowded with bees in a scarce time of honey is insufficient to bring out the swarm; neither is an abundance of honey sufficient, without the bees and the brood.

But when all of these happen together, and remain long enough, a swarm will usually occur.

These causes then appear to produce, generally begun, (sometimes when only half full, but usually remain as rudiments till the next year, when the foregoing conditions of the stock may require their use).

STATE OF QUEEN'S CELL WHEN USED

A few Queen cells are produced even before the hive is filled. They are about half finished when they receive the eggs, And as these eggs hatch into larvae, others are begun, receiving eggs several days later.

The sealing of these cells signals when you can expect the first swarm. It will generally issue the first fair day after one or more are finished.

EMPTY HIVES TO BE READY

Let's suppose that some of your stocks are ready to swarm. And we will also presume that your empty hives are ready for the reception of swarms before hand.

The first indication of a swarm will be an unusual number of bees around the entrance, from one to sixty minutes before they start. Confusion seems to prevail, with bees running about in every direction; the entrance apparently closed with the mass of bees. Presently a column from the interior forces a passage to the open air and they come rushing out by the hundreds, all vibrating their wings as they march out. When a few inches from the entrance, they rise into the air.

At first, the bees describe circles of few feet, but as they recede they spread over an area of several yards. Their movement is much slower than usual. In a few minutes thousands are seen revolving in every possible direction!

Once out of the hive, the bees select the branch of a

tree or a bush. Within five to ten minutes, all the bees have clustered in a body at the spot indicated.

These bees should be hived immediately, for they show impatience if left too long in the sun.

MANNER OF HIVING

It makes little difference what way they are put in the hive. Proceed as is most convenient. An old table or bench is good to keep them out of the grass. Or you can lay your bottom-board on the ground, make it level, set your hive on it, and raise one edge an inch or more to give the bees a chance to enter.

USUAL METHOD

Cut off the branch with the bees, if it can be done, and shake it in front of the hive. Some of the bees will discover it, and commence a vibration of their wings. This is kept up until all are inside the new hive.

A great many bees are apt to stop at the entrance, preventing others going in. You can expedite the matter with a stick or quill, gently pushing them away so more can enter.

If this gentle means does not induce the obstinate bees to go in, a little water sprinkled on them will facilitate operations greatly when nothing else will. (Be careful and not over-do the matter by using too much water, else they can become too wet to move at all.)

If they have clustered on a branch you do not want to cut off, place your bottom-board as near as convenient; then turn it bottom up, directly under the main part of the cluster. If you have an assistant, let him jar the branch sufficiently to detach the bees, allowing them to fall directly into the hive.

If no assistant is at hand, use the bottom of the hive to strike the under side of the branch hard enough to dislodge the bees, then turn it on the board to collect them.

WHEN OUT OF REACH

After putting the hive in its place, some of the bees may go back out. In that case, hold a small branch full of leaves directly under them. Shake it to prevent their clustering there and you will soon have them all collected, ready to bring down, and put by the hive.

If you succeed in getting nearly all the bees in the first effort, and but few are left, merely shaking the branch will be sufficient to prevent their holding fast, and will turn their attention to those below that have found the hive. As soon as it is realized that a home has been found, a buzzing commences inside, communicating that fact to those outside. These outliers will immediately turn to face the hive, and hum in concert while marching in.

ANOTHER PLAN

Even if a branch is fifteen feet high, you still can hive your swarming bees. Select two or three light poles of suitable length that have a branch at the upper end, large enough to hold a two-bushel basket. This is raised directly under the swarm. Then using another pole, dislodge the bees, causing them to fall into the basket. After quickly lowering the basket, throw a sheet over it to prevent the bees' escape. They soon become quiet, and may be hived without attempting to go back to the branch.

WHEN THEY CANNOT BE SHAKEN OFF

Swarms will sometimes get into places where it's impossible to jar them off, or cut off the branch. In such a case, place the hive nearby, and take a large tin dipper, scooping up bees and throwing them bees into it. As these first bees discover that a home is being provided, they will set up a call for the rest of their tribe (by vibrating their wings).

Once you get the Queen inside the hive, there is no trouble with the remainder, no matter how many are left. But if they discover that the Queen is still on the tree, they will leave the hive and cluster again.

PROTECTION FROM THE SUN

Swarms should be protected from the sun in hot weather. If the heat is oppressive and the bees cluster outside, sprinkle them with water to drive them inside the hive. Wetting the hive occasionally will make them much more comfortable.

CLUSTERING BUSHES

If there are no large trees in the vicinity of your apiary, all the better, as there will then be no threat of your swarms lighting on them. But all beekeepers are not so fortunate. In such a place it is necessary to provide something for them to cluster on.

Get some bushes six or eight feet high (hemlock is preferable); cut off the ends of the branches except a few near the top: secure the whole with strings to prevent swaying in ordinary winds; make a hole in the earth deep enough to hold them, and large enough to be lifted out easily.

The bees will be likely to cluster on some of these. They can then be raised out, and the bees hived without difficulty. A bunch of dry mullein tops tied together on the end of a pole, makes a very good place for clustering; it so nearly resembles a swarm that the bees themselves appear to be sometimes deceived. I have frequently known them leave a branch where they had begun to cluster, and settle on this when held near.

The motives for immediately removing the swarm to the stand are that they are generally more convenient to watch in case they are disposed to leave; also many bees can be saved. All that leave the hive, mark the location the same as in spring; several hundreds will probably leave the first day; a few may leave several times; when removed at night, such will return to the stand of the previous day, and generally are lost; whereas, if they are carried at once to a permanent stand, this loss is avoided.

Those bees that are left flying at the time, return to the old stock, which those that return from the swarm the next day will not always do. The time for moving them now is no more than at another. It is unnecessary to object, and say that "it will take too long to wait for the bees to get in." This will not do. I shall insist on your getting all the bees to enter.

TWO OR MORE SWARMS LIABLE TO UNITE

If we expect to keep many stocks, the chances are that two or more may issue at one time; and when they do, they nearly always cluster together (I once knew an instance where only three stocks were kept; they all swarmed and clustered together). It is plain that the greater the number of stocks, the more such chances are multiplied.

One first swarm, if of the usual size, will contain bees enough for profit, yet two such will work together without quarrelling, and will store about one-third more than either would alone; that is, if each single swarm would get 50 pounds, the two together would not get over 70 pounds, perhaps less. Here, then, is a loss of 30 pounds. You will therefore see the advantage of keeping the first swarms separate.

CAN OFTEN BE PREVENTED

"Prevention is better than cure." We can, if we keep a good lookout, often prevent more than one issuing at a time. This depends on our knowledge of indications, in a great measure.

I have said that before starting to fly off, they were about the entrance in great numbers; the first indications being a column of bees rushing from the hive.

Now, in good weather, when we have reason to expect many swarms, it is our duty to watch closely, especially when the weather has been unfavorable for several days previous. A number of stocks may have finished their Queen cells during the bad weather, and be ready to come out within the first hour of sunshine in the middle of the day.

Even if nothing unusual is seen about the entrance, raise the cover to the boxes. If the bees in them are all quiet as usual, no swarm need be immediately apprehended, and you will probably have time to hive one or two first.

But should you discover the bees running to and fro in great commotion, although there may be but few about the entrance, you should lose no time in sprinkling those outside with water from a watering pot. They will immediately enter the hive to avoid the supposed shower. In half an hour they will be ready to start again, during which time the others hopefully have been secured.

PREVENTING SWARMS FROM UNITING

When any of the subsequent swarms try to unite with those already hived, throw a sheet over the hive to keep them out.

An assistant is very important in such cases. One can watch symptoms and keep them back, while the other hives the swarms.

WHEN TWO HAVE UNITED, THE METHOD OF SEPARATING

Two or more swarms will cluster together, and not quarrel, if put in one hive; I have already told you the disadvantages. Therefore, you must divide them.

First, get two empty hives and divide the bees as nearly equal as possible. Generally the best way is to spread a sheet on the ground and shake the bees into the center. Set the hives on each side of the mass, their edges raised to allow the bees to enter. If too many are disposed to enter one hive, set it farther off.

If they cluster where they cannot be got to the earth in a body, they must be dipped off as before directed, but, in this case, putting a dipper full in each hive alternately, until all are in.

They should be made to hurry some in going in; keep the entrance clear, and stir them up often. Sprinkle very little water on them, as they should not be allowed to stop their humming until all are in.

We have one chance in two of getting a Queen in each. The two hives should now be placed twenty feet apart; if there is a Queen in each, the bees in both will remain quiet, and the work is done. But if not, the bees in the one destitute will soon manifest it by running about in all directions, and, when the Queen cannot be found, will leave for the other hive, where there are probably two.

Now there are two or three methods of separating these Queens.

One is, to empty the bees out and proceed as before, a kind of chance game, that may succeed at the next trial, and may have to be repeated.

Another way is, that, as soon as it is ascertained which is without a Queen, before many bees leave, spread down a sheet, set the hive on it, and tie the corners over the top to secure the bees for the present. Turn the hive on its side to give them air. When this division is secured, get another hive, and jar out those with the Queens; let them enter as before, and then set them apart, etc., watching the result; if the Queens are not yet separate,

it will be known by the same appearances. The process must be continued till separate, or the number with the Queens may be easily looked over, and one of them found; indeed, a sharp lookout should be kept up from the beginning, and the Queens caught, if possible.

NO DANGER OF A STING BY THE QUEEN

No danger of a sting, as the Queen will not demean herself to use that for a common foe. She saves that for a *royal* antagonist.

When successful in obtaining a Queen, put her in a tumbler or some safe place, then put your bees in two hives, place them as directed, and you will soon learn where your Queen is needed.

After all is done, the two hives should not be nearer than twenty feet, at least the first day; perhaps forty would be still better. When two swarms are mixed, and then separated, it is evident that a portion of each swarm must be in both hives. A Queen in each must of course be a stranger to at least a part of the bees; these might, if their own mother was too near, discover her, and leave the stranger for an old acquaintance, and, in the act of going, take the whole colony with them.

SOME PRECAUTIONS IN HIVING TWO SWARMS TOGETHER

If you are disposed to separate them, but are afraid to work among them to this extent in the middle of the day, or if there is danger of more issuing, to mix with them, and add to your perplexity, of which you already have enough, then you can hive them as a single swarm; but, instead of a bottom-board, invert an empty hive and set the one with the swarm on this, and insert a wedge between them, for ventilation. As many bees are liable to drop down, in this case the lower hive will catch them, and there is less danger of leaving. Let them remain till near sunset, when another course may be taken to find a Queen, though by that time one is sometimes killed.

First, look into the lower hive for a dead Queen, and, if none is found, look thoroughly for a little compact cluster of bees, about the size of a hen's egg. Secure this cluster in a tumbler; it is quite sure one of the Queens is a prisoner in the middle. (Should two clusters be seen, get both.) Then divide the bees, and give the destitute group a Queen.

Or, if you have two, one to each, it would be wise to see if the Queens are alive by removing the bees from about each of them. Should you find nothing of the kind, spread a sheet on the ground, shake the bees on one end of it, and set the hive on the other. They will immediately begin a march for the hive. You may now see the cluster, but they will spread out in marching, and give you a good chance to identify her majesty. A tumbler is the most convenient thing to set over her. No matter if a few bees are shut up with her. By this time you know what to do next.

SWARMS SOMETIMES RETURN

Occasionally a swarm will issue, and in a few minutes return to the old stock. The most common cause is the inability of the old Queen to fly, on account of her burden of eggs, old age, or something else. I have sometimes, after the swarm had returned found the Queen near the stock, and put her back, and the next day she would come out again, and fly without difficulty (perhaps she had discharged some of her eggs).

Returning is more frequent in windy weather, or when the sun is partially obscured by clouds. Sometimes they will not re-issue until a young Queen is matured, eight or ten days afterwards; and a few, not at all. But when the Queen returns with the swarm, they usually come out again the next day, or day after.

REPETITION PREVENTED

Sometimes a swarm will issue and return three or four days in succession, often owing to some inability of the Queen. Frequently she will be found while the swarm is leaving outside the hive, unable to fly.

In such cases it is only necessary to have a tumbler ready, and watch for her; and as soon as she appears, secure her. Then get an empty hive ready for the swarm, a sheet, and put down a bottom-board a few feet from the stock. When the swarm comes back, the first bees that alight on the hive will set up the call. As soon as this is perceived, lose no time in setting the old stock on the board and throwing the sheet over it to keep out the bees. Put the new one in its place on the stand, with the Queen in it, In a few minutes the swarm will be in the *new* hive.

But should the swarm begin to cluster in a convenient place, when you have so caught the Queen, by being expeditious she may be put with the swarm, before they have missed her and may be hived in the usual way.

Basics of ... Beekeeping

CHAPTER FIFTEEN

ARTIFICIAL SWARMS

Artificial swarms can be made with safety at the proper season. For the beekeeper who wishes to increase his stocks, it will be an advantage to understand some of the principles involved in creating a *forced swarm*.

INDUCING A SWARM

A populous hive, rich in stores, can be induced to swarm by the following process:

During the season for natural swarming, choose that part of day, 10 a.m. to 2 p.m., when the largest number of bees are likely to be abroad in the fields. If any bees are clustered in front of the hive, or on the bottom-board, puff among them a few whiffs of smoke, so as to force them to go up among the combs.

Meanwhile, have an empty hive or box in readiness, the diameter of which is the same as that of the hive from which you intend to drive the swarm.

Lift the hive very gently, and without the slightest jar, from its bottom-board; invert it and carry it a short distance from its old stand, as bees are always much more inclined to be peaceable in an unfamiliar spot.

If the hive is carefully placed on the ground, upside down, scarcely a single bee will fly out, and there will be little danger of being stung. Timid and inexperienced apiarians will, of course, protect themselves with a protective bee suit, and they may have an assistant to sprinkle the hive gently with sugar water as soon as it is inverted.

After placing the hive in an inverted position on the ground, place the empty hive over it, plugging every crack from which a bee might escape with paper.

Tap the hive sharply on the front and back. These rappings produce a most decided effect on the bees: their first impulse is to sally out and wreak their vengeance upon those who have thus rudely assailed their honeyed dome. But as soon as they find that they are shut in, a sudden fear that they are going to be driven from their treasures seems to take possession of them. They busily engage in gorging themselves with honey. Nearly every bee will fill itself to its utmost capacity, in preparation for a forced emigration. A prodigious hum can be heard as the bees begin to mount into the upper box.

In about ten minutes from the time the rapping began, the mass of the bees with their Queen will have ascended, and will hang clustered, just like a natural swarm.

The box with the expelled bees must now be gently lifted off, and should be placed upon a bottom-board with a gauze wire ventilator, assuring that the confined bees will have plenty of air. If no gauze wire bottom-board is at hand, the hive must be wedged up, so as to admit an abundance of air, and be set in a shady place.

The hive from which the bees were driven should now be set on its old spot, so all the bees returning from abroad may enter it. As soon as the opportunity is given them, they will crowd into their well-known home, and if there are no royal cells started they will proceed almost at once to construct them. And the next day they will act as though the forced swarm had left of its own accord.

If this procedure takes place during the season for natural swarming, the hive will contain immature Queens. Thus, a new Queen will soon take the place of the old one, just as in natural swarming.

DIVIDING THE HIVES

Instead of trying to make an equitable division at the time of driving out the bees, I prefer to expel all that I can, and to rely upon the bees returning from their gatherings, to replenish the old stock. If the number appears to be too small, I open temporarily the entrance of the hive containing the forced swarm, and permit as many as I judge best, to come out and enter their old abode.

It must here be borne in mind, that bees which are thus ejected from a hive, do not, in all respects, act like a natural swarm, which having left the parent stock, of its own accord, never seeks, unless it has lost its Queen, to return. Whereas, many of the forced swarm, as soon as they leave the hive into which they have been driven, will return to their former abode. The same is true of bees which are moved to any distance not far enough to be beyond the limits of their previous excursions in search of food.

Having ascertained that the parent hive contains a sufficient number of bees to carry on operations, about sunset, after the bees are all at home, it may be removed to a new stand.

Then the expelled colony must be placed precisely where the hive from which they were driven stood, and have their liberty restored to them. The next morning, they will work with as much vigor as though they had swarmed in the natural way.

SOME OBJECTIONS

It has been argued by some that "nature is the best guide, and it is better to let the bees have their own way about swarming – if honey is abundant, and the stock is in condition to spare a swarm, their own instincts will teach them to construct royal cells; if it fails before they are ready, and the royal brood is destroyed, it is because the existence of the swarm would be precarious, and it is best not to issue."

But yet, we are sometimes anxious to increase our stocks to the utmost that safety will allow, and often have some hives that can spare a swarm as well as not, but refuse to leave.

By taking the matter into our own hands, we make a sure thing of it. That is, we are sure to get the swarms, when if left to the bees it would be uncertain. And afterwards we see no difference between artificial or natural swarms of equal size.

Basics of ... Beekeeping

Introducing a new Queen.

CHAPTER SIXTEEN

SWARMS THAT LOSE THEIR QUEEN

Swarms that lose their Queen the first few hours after being hived, generally return to the parent stock; with the exception that they sometimes unite with some other.

However, some bees who disperse to other hives are met with a very unkind reception. As a general rule, a bee with a load of freshly gathered honey is almost always welcomed by any hive to which he may carry his treasures; while a poor unfortunate that ventures to present itself empty and poverty stricken, is generally at once destroyed!

A SUGGESTION AND AN ANSWER

It has been suggested as a profitable speculation, "to hive a large swarm without a Queen, and give them a piece of brood-comb containing eggs, to rear one, and then as soon as it is matured, deprive them of it, giving them another piece of comb, and continue it throughout the summer, putting on boxes for surplus honey. The bees having no young brood to consume any honey, no time will be lost, or taken to nurse them, and as a consequence they will be enabled to store large quantities of surplus honey."

This appears very plausible, and to a person without experience somewhat conclusive. If success depended on some animal whose lease of life was a little longer, it would answer better to calculate in this way. But as a bee seldom sees the anniversary of its birthday, and most of them perish the first few months of their existence, it is bad economy. It will be found that the largest amount of our surplus honey is obtained from our prolific stocks. Therefore it is all-important that every swarm and stock has a Queen to repair this constant loss.

BEES TAKE NO CHANCES

Instinct teaches the bee to make the matters left to them as nearly a *sure bet* as possible.

When they want one Queen, they raise half a dozen.

If only half a dozen Drones were reared, the chances of the Queen meeting one in the air would be very much reduced. But when a thousand are in the air instead of one, the chances are a thousand times multiplied.

If a stock casts a swarm, there is a young Queen to be impregnated, and be got safely back, or the stock is lost. Every time she leaves, there is a chance of her being lost. If the number of Drones was any less than it is, the Queen would have to repeat her excursions in proportion, before successful. As it is, some have to leave several times. The chances and consequences are so great, that on the whole no doubt but it is better to rear a thousand unnecessarily, than to lack one just in time of need. Therefore let us endeavor to be content with the present arrangement, inasmuch as we could not better it, and probably had we been consulted, would have so fixed "the thing, that it would not go at all."

But what is the use of the Drones in hives that do not swarm, and do not intend it, situated in a large room or very large hives? Such circumstances seldom produce swarms, yet as regular as the return of summer, a brood of

Drones appear. What are they for? Suppose the old Queen in such hive dies, leaving eggs or young larvae, and a young Queen is reared to supply her place. How is she to be impregnated without the Drones? Perhaps they are taught that whenever they can afford it, they should have some on hand to be ready for an emergency. I have already said when bees are numerous, and honey abundant, they never fail to provide them.

QUEEN LIABLE TO BE LOST IN EXCURSIONS

This excursion of the Queen usually takes place a little after the middle of the day, when the Drones were out in the greatest numbers. Sometimes Queens are lost on these occasions from some cause.

At times she perishes from entering the wrong hive. This is another good reason for not packing stocks too close. Hives are very often nearly alike in color and appearance. The Queen, coming out for the first time in her life, is no doubt confused by this similarity.

INDICATIONS OF THE LOSS

The next morning after a loss of this kind has occurred, and occasionally at evening, the bees may be seen running about in the greatest consternation, outside, to and fro on the sides. Some will fly off a short distance and return; one will run to another, and then to another, still in hopes, no doubt, of finding their lost sovereign!

A neighboring hive close by, on the same bench, will probably receive a portion, which will seldom resist an accession under such circumstances. All this will be going on while other hives are quiet. Towards the middle of the day, this confusion will become less marked; but the next morning it will be exhibited again, though not so plainly, and cease after the third day, when they become apparently reconciled to their fate.

They will continue their labors as usual, bringing in pollen and honey.

THE RESULT
The number of bees will gradually decrease, and be all gone by the early part of winter, leaving a good supply of honey, and an extra quantity of beebread, because there has been no young brood to consume it.

When but few bees are left, and the combs are unprotected, a moth might deposit her eggs on them, and the worms soon finish up the whole.

But in most instances, the bees from the other stocks will remove the honey for themselves.

AGE OF BEES INDICATED
Hundreds of beekeepers lose some of their stocks in this way, and can assign no reasonable cause. "Why?" say they, "Only a short time before, the hive was full of bees; I got three good swarms from it, and it always had been first rate, but all at once the bees were gone. I don't understand it!"

Such beekeepers cannot understand how rapidly a family of bees diminishes when there is no Queen to replenish it with young.

REMEDY
When you discover the loss of a Queen, the first thing

to do is ascertain if there is any after swarm to be expected from another stock (by listening for the piping). If so, wait till it issues, and then obtain a Queen from that for your stock.

Should no such swarm be indicated, go to a stock that has issued a first swarm; smoke it and find a royal cell inside. Cut it out with a broad knife, being careful not to injure it. This must now be secured in the other hive in its natural position, the lower end free from any obstacle that would interfere with the new Queen leaving it.

In a few hours the bees will secure it permanently to the combs with wax.

Soon after this royal cell is introduced, the bees are quiet. In a few days it hatches, and they have a Queen as perfect as if one of their own rearing.

MARK THE DATE OF SWARMS ON THE HIVE

It sometimes happens that a Queen will be lost at the end of the swarming season, when no other stock contains royal cells. I then look around for the poorest stock that I have on hand, one that I can afford to sacrifice, to determine if it possesses a Queen to replace the one that was lost.

OBTAINING QUEEN FROM WORKER BROOD

There is yet another method to consider. That is to obtain a piece of brood-comb containing Workers' eggs, or very young larvae. You can generally find this without much trouble in a young swarm that is making combs; the lower ends usually contain eggs. Using smoke, take a piece from one of the middle sheets, two or three inches long.

Basics of ... Beekeeping

Invert the hive that is to receive it, put the piece edgewise between the combs, spreading them apart just enough for the purpose. They will nearly always rear several Queens.

The sooner a young Queen can take the place of the old one in maternal duties, the less time will be lost in breeding, the more bees there will be to defend the combs from the moth, and the surest guaranty for surplus honey.

Basics of ... Beekeeping

CHAPTER SEVENTEEN

PRUNING

When using skep and box hives with fixed combs, good management advises removing a portion of the combs, an operation called pruning. This process trims out old honeycombs, allowing the bees to build new ones.

WHEN TO PRUNE

The old Queen leaves with the first swarm; all the eggs she leaves in the Worker-cells will be matured in about twenty-one days. Consequently this is the time to clear out the old combs with the least waste. A few Drones will be found in the cells, that would require a few days more to hatch, but these are of no account. Also a few very young larvae and some eggs may be sometimes found, the product of the young Queen; these few must be wasted, but as the bees have expended no labor upon them as yet, it is better to sacrifice these than the greater number left by her mother, which have consumed their portion of food. The bees have sealed them up, and now only require the necessary time to mature, to make a valuable addition to the stock.

Should this operation be put off, the young Queen will so fill the combs again as to make it a serious loss. Therefore, I wish to urge strongly attention to this point at the proper season.

Some recommend taking only a part of the combs, say one-third or half, in a single season, thereby taking two or three years to renew the combs. This is advisable only when the family is very small. As this space made by pruning cannot be filled without wax and labor, our surplus honey will be proportionate to its extent.

Now suppose we take out half the old combs, and get half a yield of box honey this year, and the same next, or make a full operation of it and get none this year, and a full one next. What is the difference? There is none in point of honey, but some in trouble, and that is in favor of a full operation at once. We have to go through with about the same trouble to get one-third or half as to take the whole.

STOCKS PRUNED NOW ARE BETTER FOR WINTER

Besides the advantage of saving a large brood by pruning at this season, such stocks will usually refill before fall, and are much better for wintering, which is not the case when it is done later. We must of necessity then waste the brood, and have a large space unoccupied with combs through the winter. Few combs can be made then, and those at the expense of their winter stores, unless we resort to feeding.

Furthermore, it is best to have the bees out of the way during this operation. It's much more difficult to drive the bees out of a hive in the cool weather of March or April, than in summer. They prefer warm quarters to a cold hive.

METHOD FOR PRUNING

When the combs need removing, I prefer the following method of pruning:

The first step is to blow some smoke under the hive,

depriving the bees of all disposition to sting and causing them to retreat up among the combs. Now raise the hive from the stand and carefully turn it bottom upwards, avoiding any jar, as some of the bees that were in the top when the smoke was introduced will come to the bottom to ascertain the cause of the disturbance. A whiff of smoke will immediately return them to the top.

To get the bees out of the way for pruning, take an empty hive the size of the old one, and set it over, stopping the holes; now strike the lower hive with a hammer or stick, lightly and rapidly, until nearly all the bees are in the upper hive, and set that on the stand.

The best time to do this is a little before night. It will only take about an hour.

TOOLS FOR CUTTING OUT THE COMB

The broad cutting tool is very readily made from a piece of an old scythe, about 18 inches long, by any blacksmith, by simply taking off the back, and forming a shank for a handle at the heel. The end should be ground all on one side, and square across like a carpenter's chisel. This is for cutting down the sides of the hive; the level will keep it close the whole length, when you wish to remove all the combs; it being square instead of pointed or rounded, no difficulty will be found in guiding it – and being very thin, no combs are mashed by crowding.

The other tool is for cutting off combs at the top or any other place. It is merely a rod of steel three-eighths of an inch diameter, about two feet long, with a thin blade at right angles, one and a half inches long, and a quarter inch wide, both edges sharp, upper side beveled, bottom flat, etc. You will find these tools very convenient; be sure and get them by all means; the cost cannot be compared to the advantages.

CUTTING THE COMBS

Using these tools, remove the brood-combs from the center of the hive. The combs near the top and outside are used but little for breeding, and are generally filled with honey; these should be left as a good start for refilling, but take out all that is necessary, while you are about it; then reverse the hives, putting the one containing the bees under the other; by the next morning all are up; now put it on the stand.

OBJECTION TO PRUNING

The objection to this mode of renewing combs is usually the fear of getting stung. But there is little danger, not as much as to walk among the hives on a warm day. Only begin the process right by using smoke to tame the bees. Then work carefully, without pinching them, and you will escape unhurt.

HOW OFTEN TO PRUNE

Bear in mind the disadvantages already given for too frequently renewing combs: The little value of combs for storing honey, *for our use*, after being once used for breeding; the necessity of the bees using them as long as they possibly will answer; and not compel them to be filling the hive when they might be storing honey of the purest quality in boxes, etc.

It is important that the bees should devote their whole attention to rearing brood, and be ready to cast their swarms as early as possible. One early swarm is worth two late ones. Suppose a stock is compelled to expend its honey and labor in secreting wax and constructing combs before it can proceed with breeding? Not good. Collecting food and nursing its young would better serve its future,

Basics of ... Beekeeping

CHAPTER EIGHTEEN

AVOIDING DISEASED STOCK

Bees get sick too. A few newspaper discussions are about all that have yet appeared on this subject. A distraught beekeeper was quoted in the *N.E. Farmer*: "Since the potato rot commenced, I have lost one-fourth of my stocks annually, by this disease." He adds his fears that "this race of insects will become extinct from this cause, if not arrested."

MY OWN EXPERIENCE

One of my best stocks cast no swarm through the summer; and now, instead of being crowded with bees, it contained but very few. What was the matter?

An examination revealed the following circumstances: Nine-tenths of the breeding-cells were found to contain young bees in the larva state, stretched out at full length, sealed over, dead, black, putrid, and emitting a disagreeable stench. Now here was one link in the chain of cause and effect. I had learned why there was a scarcity of bees in the hive. What should have constituted the colony's increase in numbers had died in the cells.

What caused the death of this brood at just this stage of development? All inquiries among the beekeepers of my acquaintance were met with profound ignorance. They had "never heard of it!"

I tried pruning out all those combs containing brood, leaving only those that provided honey. This was to let the bees construct new undiseased combs for breeding. But it was no use, for these new combs were invariably filled with diseased brood!

The only thing effectual was to drive out the bee into an empty, uninfected hive. In this way, I succeeded in rearing a healthy stock. But here was a loss of all surplus honey, and a swarm or two that might have been obtained from a healthy one.

PUBLIC INQUIRY AND ANSWERS

Having so many cases of the kind, I became alarmed. So I made an inquiry through an agricultural paper as to a cause, and remedy, offering a reward for answers.

One correspondent assured me that "cold weather in spring chilling the brood was the cause." Another gentleman added, "Dead bees and filth that accumulated during winter, when suffered to remain in the spring, was the cause." Still another of them explained: "If the eggs of a fowl, at any time near the end of incubation, become chilled from any cause, it stops all further development. Bees are developed by continued heat, on the same principle, and a chill produces the same effect."

Others weighed in, concluding that cold was the culprit – the chill killing the developing larvae, and their petrification setting off an unknown contagion.

A CAUSE SUGGESTED

We are all familiar to some extent with the contagious diseases of the human family, such as smallpox, whooping cough, and measles.

To a contagion, then, I would attribute the spread of

this disease among our bees. And we must find ways to halt it, no matter whether we know its origin or not.

NOT EASILY DETECTED AT FIRST

It is very difficult to detect the first hundred or two that die in a stock. But when nine-tenths of the breeding cells hold putrid larvae, there is no problem in making out a correct diagnosis.

The bees are few and inactive. When passing the hive our olfactory are saluted with nauseous effluvia, arising from this corrupting mass. Now, if we wish, or expect to escape, the most severe penalty, our neglect must never allow this extent of progression before such a stock is removed. Therefore, we must watch for symptoms – and ascertain the presence of the disease *at the earliest moment possible.*

CARE IN SELECTING STOCK HIVES FOR WINTER

Again, after the breeding season is over, in the fall, *every stock should be thoroughly inspected, and all diseased ones condemned for stock hives.* It is better to do it, even if it should take the last one. It would pay much better to procure others instead that are healthy.

SYMPTOMS TO BE OBSERVED

As no part of the breeding season is exempt, the stocks should be carefully observed during spring, and fore part of summer, relative to increase of bees. When one or more is much behind others in this respect, make an examination immediately. The hive must be inverted, and the bees smoked out of the way. Direct your attention to the breeding cells. With a sharp-pointed knife, cut off the ends of some of the cells that appear to be the oldest.

Bear in mind that young bees are always white, until some time after they take the chrysalis state. Therefore, if a larva is found of a dark color, it is dead!

Should a dozen such be found, the stock should be condemned at once, and all the bees driven into an empty hive. (The directions for this have been given) If honey should be scarce, at the time, they should be fed.

If all my neighbors were equally careful, this disease would probably soon disappear. This is like one careless farmer allowing a noxious weed to mature seeds, to be wafted by winds on the lands of a careful neighbor, who must fortify his mind to continual vigilance, or endure the injury of a foul pest.

So the successful apiarian must be continually on the watch; it is the price of success.

PESTICIDES

Many pesticides are known to be toxic to bees. Pesticide losses can be easy to identify (sudden numbers of dead bees in front of the hive) or quite difficult, due to gradual accumulation of pesticide brought in by foraging bees. Quick-acting pesticides may deprive the hive of its foragers, dropping them in the field before they can return home.

MITES

Varroa mites are considered to be the biggest pest to honeybees worldwide. They are suspected of contributing to Colony Collapse Disorder due to their ability to transmit such diseases as Deformed Wing Virus.

DEFORMED WING VIRUS

Deformed Wing Virus is one of 18 known viruses affecting the honeybee.

It is named after what is usually the most obvious deformity it induces in the development of a honeybee pupa, shrunken and deformed wings. Symptoms include damaged appendages, particularly stubby, useless wings, shortened, rounded abdomens, discoloring, and paralysis of the legs and wings.

Facing shortened lifespans (less than 48 hours), bees afflicted with DWV are typically expelled from the hive.

VIRAL DISEASES

Viral diseases afflicting honeybees include Chronic paralysis virus, Acute bee paralysis virus, Israeli acute paralysis virus, Kashmir bee virus, Black queen cell virus, Cloudy wing virus, Sacbrood virus, Kakugo virus, Invertebrate iridescent virus type 6, and Tobacco ringspot virus, among others.

BACTERIAL DISEASES

The various bacterial diseases that pose threats to honeybees include American foulbrood and European foulbrood. Spore-based American foulbrood is the most destructive of bee blood disorders.

FUNGAL DISEASES

The fungal diseases include Chalkbrood and

Stonebrood. Chalkbrood causes starvation as the fungus competes with the larva for food. A disease caused by *Aspergillus* fungi, Stonebrood produces mummification of the brood of a honeybee colony.

Basics of ... Beekeeping

CHAPTER NINETEEN

ENEMIES OF BEES

It is said the enemies of bees include rats, mice, birds, toads, and other insects. But some of these are probably clear of any actual mischief.

People might top the list. With our pesticides, cell phone transmissions, and destruction of whole bees swarms for their honey, I cannot list us on the side of bees.

Beekeepers should try to be.

SHORT-SIGHTED

There are some farmers, so short-sighted, that if it was in their power they would destroy a whole class of birds because some of them had picked a few cherries, or dug out a few hills of corn. When at the same time the farmer should be indebted to these same birds for devouring worms, insects, etc., that would otherwise have destroyed entire crops!

RATS AND MICE

Rats and mice are never troublesome to bees, except in cold weather. The entrances of all hives are too small to admit a rat. However, they appear to be fond of honey, and when it is accessible will eat several pounds in a short time.

Being smaller, mice will often enter the hive and make extensive depredations. Sometimes, after eating a space in the combs, they will there make their nest. The animal heat created by the bees makes a snug, warm place for a mouse's winter quarters.

There are two kinds of mice to consider: one, the common class, belonging to the house; the other the deer mouse.

The under side of the deer mouse is perfectly white, the back much lighter than the other kind. The latter rodent seems to be particularly fond of the bees, while the first appears to relish the honey.

A little care to prevent their depredations is well worthwhile. As rats and mice have so long since been condemned for being a universal plague, without a redeeming trait, I will say nothing in their favor.

BIRDS

The king-bird stands at the head of the list of depredators! With a fair trial he will be found guilty, though not so heinously criminal as many suppose.

Martins, and a kind of swallows, are said to be guilty of taking bees on some occasions.

The catbird also comes in for a share of censure. It is said "they will get right down by the hive, and pick up bees by the hundred." Yet, right in the face of this charge, I am disposed to acquit him. With the closest observation, I find him about the hive, picking up *only* young and immature bees, such as are removed from the combs and thrown out. Should an unlucky worm be in sight just then, while looking up a place for spinning a cocoon, or a moth reposing on some corner of the hive, their fate is at once decided.

Before destroying this bird, it would be well to judge by actual facts; otherwise we might "destroy a friend instead of a foe."

TOADS

A toad is discovered near the hives, and forthwith he is executed as a bee-eater. His food is probably small insects. Whoever has seen him swallow bees, must have watched closer than I ever did.

WASPS AND HORNETS

As for the frequent visits of the black-wasp in the sunny days of spring, little can be said in their favor – they tease and irritate the bees. They have frequent battles with the bees, but I never saw any bees devoured or carried off, nor even killed.

The yellow wasp, or hornet, that is around in autumn is of little account; their object is honey, which they will take when they can get it, but hornets are not apt to enter the hive among the bees.

ANTS – A WORD IN THEIR FAVOR

Ants come in for a share of condemnation. This industrious insect shall have my endeavors for a fair hearing; I think I can understand why they are so frequently accused of robbing bees. Many beekeepers are wholly ignorant, most of the time, of the real condition of their stocks. Many causes independent of ants, induce a reduction of population.

Suppose the bees are so reduced as to leave the combs unprotected, and the ants enter and appropriate some of the honey for themselves, and should the owner come along just then and see them engaged, "Ha! You are the rascals that have destroyed my bees."

The peculiar habits of the small black ants, probably give rise to a suspicion of mischief in this way. They live in communities of thousands – their nests are usually in old walls, in old timber, under stones, and in the earth. From their nests a string may be traced sometimes for yards, going after, and returning laden with food. During a spell of wet weather, such as would make the earth and many other places too damp and cold for a nest, they look out for better quarters. The top or chamber of our beehives affords shelter from rain. The animal heat from the bees renders it perfectly comfortable. How then can we blame them for choosing such a location, so completely answering all their wants?

As long as the bees are not disturbed, we can put up with it better. But the careless observer having discovered their train to and fro from their nest on the hive, exclaims: "Why, I have seen them going in a continual stream to the hive after honey;" when a little scrutiny into the matter would show that only the nest was on the top of the hive, and they were going somewhere else for food.

SPIDERS CONDEMNED

Spiders are a source of considerable annoyance to the apiarian ... as well as to the bees.

Not so much on account of the number of bees consumed,

As for their habit of spinning a web about the hive, that will occasionally take a moth, but it will probably entangle fifty bees in it also. This web is often at the hive entrance, entangling the bees as they go out and return.

Not relished as food, a bee caught in the morning is frequently untouched during the day. They often escape after repeated struggles.

WAX MOTHS

If we combine into one phalanx all the depredators yet named, and compare their ability for mischief with the wax moth, we shall find their powers of destruction but a small item! Of the moth itself we would have nothing to fear were it not for her progeny that consist of a hundred or a thousand vile worms whose food is principally wax or comb.

Basics of ... Beekeeping

The Wax Moth.

CHAPTER TWENTY
PROTECTING HONEY FROM THE MOTH

The Wax Moth (*Galleria mellonella*) a brownish moth that lays its eggs in beehives. The caterpillars cover the combs with silken tunnels and feed on beeswax. These worms can destroy a bee colony.

ABOUT THE WORMS

These little white worms are the caterpillar larvae of moths. They are difficult to keep out.

At first you might see a white dust, like flour, on the side of the combs, or on the bottom of the jar. Then as the worms grow larger, this dust gets coarser. By looking closely at the combs, a small white thread-like line is perceptible, enlarging as the worm develops.

When combs are filled with honey, the worms go only along the surface, eating nothing but the sealing of the cells; seldom penetrating to the center. Wax, and not honey, is their food.

TIME OF TRANSFORMATION

The worm, after spinning its cocoon, soon changes to a chrysalis, and remains inactive for several days, when it makes an opening in one end and crawls out. The temperature governs the time taken for this transformation, although few ever pass the winter in this state. It is a rare thing to find a moth before the end of May, and not many till the middle of June; but after this time they are more numerous till the end of the season.

FREEZING DESTROYS WORMS, COCOON AND MOTH

It is pretty well demonstrated that the moth, its eggs, larvae and chrysalis cannot pass the winter without warmth of some kind to prevent their freezing to death.

Perhaps it is impossible to winter bees without preserving some eggs of the moth or a few worms at the same time. The only place that the moth chrysalis would be safe is in the vicinity of the bees. The warmth generated by the bees will keep these eggs from freezing and preserve their vitality. When warm weather approaches in the spring, those nearest the bees are probably hatched first, and commence depredations.

STOCKS MORE LIABLE TO BE DESTROYED LAST OF SUMMER

In July and August it is different in this respect; a single moth may enter the hive and deposit several hundred eggs. But the heat from the bees is now unnecessary to hatch them. The weather at this season will make any part of the hive warm enough to set the moth's whole brood to work at once, and in three weeks all may be destroyed!

It is bad management to allow honey or combs to be devoured by this disgusting creature. A little care to know the condition of the stocks *is necessary* to prevent their getting the start.

A MOTH CAN GO WHERE BEES CAN

A mothproof hive is yet to be constructed. We frequently hear of them, but when they come to be tested, somehow these worms get where the bees are. When your hives become so full of bees that they cover the board in a cool morning, the worms will be seldom found there, except under the edge of the hive.

TRAP TO CATCH WORMS

You may now raise it, but you may still catch the worms by laying under the bees a narrow shingle, a stick of elder split in two lengthwise, and the pith scraped out, or anything else that will afford them protection from the bees, and where they may spin their cocoons. These should be removed every few days, and the worms destroyed, and the trap put back. Do not neglect it till they change to the moth, and you have nothing but to remove the empty cocoon.

BIRDHOUSE FOR WREN

Put up a birdhouse for a wren to nest in. Wrens love to eat waxworms. He would be on the lookout when you were away. The cage for him need not be more than four inches square; it should be situated as near as possible to the bees; to a post, tree, or side of some building a few feet high.

ANOTHER SOLUTION

Perhaps you may find one hive in ten with no worms in it; however, others may contain from one to twenty of the little buggers after a week or so.

They must be destroyed. To do so, allow all the eggs to

hatch, which in cool weather takes three weeks. They should be watched, making sure no worms get large enough to injure the combs before they are wiped out.

Find a large barrel that is fairly airtight. Into this put the boxes, with the holes or bottom open. In one corner place a dish to hold some sulfur matches. When all is ready, ignite the matches, and close the container for several hours.

A little care is required to get it just right: If too little sulfur is used, the worms will not be killed; if too much, it gives the combs a greenish color.

If the worms are not killed on the first trial, another dose must be administered.

Basics of ... Beekeeping

CHAPTER TWENTY-ONE
ROBBERIES

Robbing is another source of occasional loss to the apiarian. This honey is not being stolen by your neighbors, but by your neighbor's bees.

This frequently happens in the spring, at any time in warm weather when honey is scarce. It is very annoying, and sometimes gets neighbors in contention.

Many people suppose, if one person has but one stock, and another has ten, that the ten will combine for plundering the one. It is true, when one family finds another weak and defenseless, possessing treasure, they have no scruples about carrying off the last particle of honey. The hurry and bustle attending it seldom escape the notice of the other families; and when one hive has been robbed in an apiary, perhaps two-thirds of the other families, sometimes all, have participated in the plunder.

IMPROPER REMEDIES

Notwithstanding it is common to hear remarks like this: "I had a first-rate hive of bees and Mr. A.'s bees began to rob them. I tried every thing to stop it. I moved them around in several places to prevent their finding the hive. It did no good. The first I knew they were all gone – bees, honey, and all! The bees all joined the robbers."

Now the fact is, not one *good* stock of bees in fifty will ever be robbed, if the entrance is properly protected. His moving the hive was enough to ruin any stock; bees were lost at every change, until nothing was left but honey to tempt the robbers; whereas, if left on its stand, it might have escaped.

With many people, the remedies are often the cause of the disease. The most fatal is, of course, to move the hive a few yards; another, to close the hive entirely (very liable to smother them); or, break out some comb and set the honey to running.

DIFFICULTY IN DECIDING

There is nothing about the apiary more difficult to determine than whether your hive is being robbed. All the culprits and protectors look alike.

It is generally supposed than when a number of bees are outside fighting, it is conclusive they are also robbing ... which is seldom the case. On the contrary, a show of resistance indicates a strong colony, and that they are disposed to defend their treasures. I have no fears for a stock that has courage to repel an attack.

We find the most danger with weak families that show no resistance. In seasons of scarcity, all *good* colonies keep sentinels about the entrance, whose duty it is to examine every bee that attempts to enter. If it is a member of the community, it is allowed to pass; if not, it is examined on the spot. It would seem that a password was requisite for admittance, for no sooner does a stranger-bee endeavor to get in, than it is known. There is no delay; no waiting for witnesses for defense. Each bee is a qualified jurist, judge, and executioner. The more a bee attempts to escape, the more likely it will be to receive a sting.

THEIR BATTLES

In the spring I have frequently seen the whole front side of the hive covered with buzzing combatants. Several will surround one stranger; one or two will bite its legs, another the wings; another will make a feint of stinging, while another is ready to take what honey it has.

Sometimes the trespassing bee is allowed to go after yielding all its honey. But at other times it might be dispatched with a sting, which is almost instantly fatal.

A bee is killed sooner by a sting than any other means, except crushing. Maybe a leg will tremble for a minute; the legs are drawn close to the body; the abdomen contracts to half its usual size, unless filled with honey.

The only places the sting will penetrate a bee are the joints of the abdomen, legs, the neck, etc. I have occasionally seen one bee drag about the dead body of its victim, being unable to withdraw its sting from a joint in the leg.

During the fight, a few bees may be seen buzzing around in search of a unguarded entrance to the hive. If one is found, the bee alights and enters it in search of honey. At other times, when about to enter, the invader meets a soldier on duty, and is on the wing again in an instant.

But another time may prove more unfortunate, the bee getting nabbed by a guard. Then it must either break away, or suffer the penalty of insect justice, which is generally fatal.

BAD POLICY TO RAISE THE HIVES

A great many apiarians raise their hives an inch from

the board early in spring. They seem to disregard the chance it gives robbers to enter on every side. It is like setting the door of your own house open, to tempt the thief, and then complain of his depravity.

THE ROBBER'S M.O.

Each robber, when leaving the hive, instead of flying in a direct line to its home, will turn its head towards the hive to mark the spot, that it may know where to return for another load, in the same manner that they do when leaving their hive in the spring. The first time the young bees leave home, they mark their location, by the same process.

A DUTY

It is the duty of every beekeeper who expects to succeed, to know which of his stocks are weak. An examination can be made by turning the hive bottom up, and letting the sun among the combs. The number of inhabitants in them is easily seen. When weak, close the entrance till there is just room for one bee to pass at a time.

On the first pleasant days, before honey is obtained plentifully, a little after noon, look out for robbers to commence their invasion. Whenever a weak stock shows a fit of unusual activity, it is quite certain you are observing either robbers or young bees; the difficulty is to decide which.

Their motions are alike, but there is a little difference in color – the young bees are a shade lighter; the abdomen of the robbers, filled with honey, are a little larger. It requires close observation to determine which is which.

A TEST

But while you're learning this nice distinction, your bees may be ruined.

We will, therefore, offer some other means of protection for your honey.

Bees, when they have been stealing a sack of honey from a neighboring hive, will generally run several inches from the entrance before flying: kill some of these; if filled with honey, they are robbers; because it is very suspicious, to be filled with honey when leaving the hive.

ROBBING USUALLY COMMENCES ON A WARM DAY

Unless it should be cool, the robbers will continue their operations till evening. Very often some are unable to get home in the dark, and become lost.

This, by the way, is another good test of robbing. Visit the hives every warm evening. The robbers commence depredations on the warmest days; seldom otherwise. If any are at work when honest laborers should be at home, they need attention.

REMEDIES

The least trouble is to remove the weak hive to the cellar, or some dark, cool place, for a few days, until at least two or three warm days have passed, that the robbers may abandon the search.

They will then probably attack the stock on the next stand.

Basics of ... Beekeeping

A CASE IN POINT

Having been away from home a couple of days, I found, on my return, a swarm of medium strength that had been carelessly exposed. Their hive had been plundered of about fifteen pounds of honey, every particle it had. The usual number of bees lingered among the combs, to all appearance, very disconsolate. I at once removed them to the cellar, and fed them for a few days.

After the robbers gave up looking for more plunder, the hive was returned to the stand, its entrance nearly closed. In a short time it built up a valuable stock; but had I'd left it a day longer, it probably wouldn't have been worth a straw.

FURTHER DIRECTIONS

When a stock has been removed, if the next stand contains a weak, instead of a strong one, it is best to take that hive in also. It will be returned to the stand as soon as the robbers will allow it.

Another method, when you are *sure* a stock is being robbed, I to wait till there are as many plunderers inside as you can get, then close up the hive, trapping them inside. Carry it in, and wait two or three days. When you set them out again, you'll discover that the strange bees will have join the weak family, and are as eager to defend what is now *their* treasure as they were before to carry it off.

This principle of "forgetting home and uniting with others," after a lapse of a few days, can be used effectively in cases like this. It succeeds about four times in five. Weak stocks are strengthened in this way very easily; and the shanghaied bees are hardly missed by the original

Lorenzo Lorraine Langstroth

tribes.

The trick is to know when you've trapped enough bees to be about equal to the weak stock. If too few of the strangers are enclosed, they surely will be destroyed.

Basics of ... Beekeeping

CHAPTER TWENTY-TWO
MELTING DOWN OF COMBS

When extreme hot weather occurs immediately after the bees have gathered a plentiful harvest, the wax composing a new comb is very liable to become softened, until it breaks loose from its fastenings and settles to the bottom of the hive.

Sometimes the injury is trifling, only a piece or two slipping down; at other times the whole contents fall in a confused and broken mass, the weight pressing out the honey, and besmearing the bees. When something like that happens, the confused bees creep out of the hive and fly away in every direction.

FIRST INDICATIONS
The first indications of such an accident will be spotting the bees outside in clusters, when the hive is perhaps only half or two-thirds full, with honey running out from the bottom (this is when part has fallen).

AFTERMATH
When the hive is nearly full, and only one or two sheets melt down, the lower edge will rest on the floor, with the other combs keeping it in an upright position, until the bees fasten it again. It is generally as well to leave such pieces as they are.

If the hive is but half full, and such pieces are not kept perpendicular by the remaining combs, they are apt to be broken and crushed badly, and most of the honey will be wasted. To save this, it will be necessary to remove the pieces of comb.

Some of the bees are likely to have been crushed, but the majority will have escaped, even covered with honey. After cleaning it off they will be in working order.

The good news: After the first year combs become thicker, and are not so liable to give way.

PREVENTION

To prevent such occurrences, ventilate the hive by raising it on little blocks at the corners. Also protect the hive from the sun; and, if necessary, wet the outside with *cold* water.

When this happened to one of my hives, I kept the young bees wet through the middle of the day, and I have no doubt but I saved several by this means. However, a piece or two of honeycomb had come down, spilling just enough honey to attract other bees. It was not safe to close the hive to prevent robbers, as this would have made the heat still greater, and been certain destruction of the stock.

The best protection I found was to put a few stems of asparagus around the bottom of the hive. While allowing free circulation of air, this made it difficult for the robbers to approach the entrance without first creeping through this hedge and encountering some bees that belonged to the hive, With this assistance, my bees were able to defend themselves till all the wasting honey was taken up.

Basics of ... Beekeeping

CHAPTER TWENTY-FOUR

WINTERING BEES

In our climate of great and sudden extremes, many colonies are annually injured or destroyed by undue exposure to heat or cold.

In summer, thin hives are often exposed to the direct heat of the sun, so that the combs melt, and the bees are drowned in their own sweets. Even if they escape utter ruin, they cannot work to advantage in the almost suffocating heat of their hives.

But in those places where the winters are both long and severe, it is much more difficult to protect the bees from the cold than from the heat. Bees are not, as some suppose, in a *dormant*, or *torpid* condition in winter. It must be remembered that they were intended to live in colonies, in winter, as well as summer.

The wasp, hornet, and other insects which do not live in families in the winter, lay up no stores for cold weather, and are so organized as to be able to endure in a torpid state, a very low temperature; so low that it would be certain death to a honeybee, which when frozen, is as surely killed as a frozen man.

As soon as the temperature of the hives falls too low for their comfort, the bees gather themselves into a more compact body to preserve their animal heat. And if the cold becomes so great that this will not suffice, they keep up an incessant, tremulous motion, accompanied by a loud humming noise. In other words, they undertake active exercise in order to keep warm! If a thermometer is pushed up among them, it will indicate a high temperature, even when the external atmosphere is many degrees below zero. When the bees are unable to maintain the necessary amount of animal heat, an occurrence that is very common with small colonies in badly protected hives, then, as a matter of course, they will perish.

Extreme cold, when of long continuance, very frequently destroys colonies in thin hives, even when they are strong both in bees and honey. The inside of such hives is often filled with frost, and the bees, after eating all the food in the combs in which they are clustered, are unable to enter the frosty combs, and thus starve in the midst of plenty.

Every year, the winter's cold causes many of the most flourishing stocks to perish by starvation. The extra quantity of food that they are compelled to eat, in order to keep up their heat in their miserable hives, is often the turning point with them between life and death. Sadly, they starve, when with proper protection, they would have had food enough and to spare.

BEES IN COLD WEATHER

We will first endeavor to examine the condition of a stock left to nature, without any care, and see if it affords any hints for our guidance, when to assist and protect with artificial means.

Warmth being the first requisite, a family of bees at the approach of cold weather crowd together in a globular form, into a compass corresponding to the degree of cold; when at zero it is much less than at thirty above. Those on the outside of this cluster are somewhat stiffened with cold; while those inside are as brisk and lively as in summer. In severe weather every possible space within their circle is occupied; even each cell not containing pollen or honey will hold a bee.

Suppose this cluster is sufficiently compact for mutual warmth, with the mercury at 40, and a sudden change brings it down to zero, in a few hours, this body of bees, like most other things, speedily contracts by the cold. The bees on the outside, being already chilled, a portion of them that does not keep up with the shrinking mass, is left exposed at a distance from their fellows, and receive but little benefit of the warmth generated there; they part with their vitality, and are lost.

WINTER IN THE HIVE

Bee's winter quarters are among the brood combs, where the hatching of the brood leaves most of the cells empty; and the space between the combs is half an inch; a wise and beautiful arrangement; as ten times the number of bees can pack themselves within a circle of six inches, as can in the other case; and in consequence the same number of bees can secure much more animal heat, and endure the cold much better; but a *small* family, even here, will often be found frozen, as well as starving.

FROST AND ICE SOMETIMES SMOTHER BEES

Besides freezing, there are other facts to be observed in stocks that stand in the cold. If we examine the interior of a hive containing a medium-sized swarm, on the first severely cold morning, we shall find the combs and sides of the hive covered with a white frost.

In the middle of the day, or as soon as the temperature is slightly raised, this begins to melt, – first next to the bees, then at the sides. A succession of cold nights will prevent the evaporation of this moisture; and this process of freezing and thawing, at the end of a week or two, will form icicles sometimes as large as a man's finger, attached to the combs and the sides of the hive. When the bottom of the hive is close to the floor, it forms a sealing around the edges, perfectly airtight, and your bees are smothered.

FROST MAY CAUSE STARVATION

Frost is frequently the cause of medium or small families starving in cold weather, even when there is plenty of honey in the hive. Suppose all the honey in the immediate vicinity of the cluster of bees is exhausted, and, the combs in every direction from them are covered with frost; if a bee should leave the mass and venture among them for a supply, its fate would be as certain as starvation. And without timely intervention of warmer weather, they *must* perish!

TOO MUCH HONEY MAY SOMETIMES BE STORED

After the flowers fail, and all the brood has matured and left the combs, it sometimes happens that a stock has an opportunity of plundering, and rapidly filling all those cells that had been occupied with brood during the yield of honey, and which then effectually prevents their storing in them.

This, then, prevents close packing, which is all-important for warmth.

Although a large family, as much care is needed as with the smaller ones. Also such as are affected with diseased brood should receive extra attention for the same reason.

TIME FOR SETTING OUT BEES

The time for carrying out bees is generally in March. A warm pleasant day is the best, and one quite cold, better than one only *moderately* warm.

After their long confinement, the light attracts them out at once, (unless very cold air prevents), and if the rays of a warm sun do not keep them active, they will soon be chilled and lost.

Some beekeepers take out their stocks at evening. If we could be always sure of having the next day a fair one, it would probably be the best time; but should it be only moderate, or cloudy, it would be attended with considerable loss – or if the next day should be quite cold, but few would leave, and then the only risk would be to get *a good day*, before one that was just warm enough to make them leave the hive, but not quite enough to enable them to return.

NOT TOO MANY STOCKS TAKEN OUT AT ONCE

When too many are taken out at once, the rush from all the hives is so much like a swarm that it appears to confuse them. Some of the stocks by this means will get more bees than actually belong to them, while others are proportionally short, which is unprofitable, and to equalize them is some trouble; yet it can be done. Being all wintered in one room, the scent or the means of distinguishing their own family from strangers, becomes so much alike, that they mix together without contention.

FAMILIES MAY BE EQUALIZED

By taking advantage of this immediately, or before the scent has again changed, and each hive has something peculiar to *itself*, you can change the stands of very weak and very strong families.

To prevent, as far as possible, some of these bad effects, I prefer waiting for a fair day to begin, sufficiently warm to make it safe from chill.

SNOW NEED NOT ALWAYS PREVENT CARRYING OUT BEES

I am not particular about the snow being gone – if it has only lain long enough to have melted a part of it, it is "terra firma" to a bee, and answers equally well as the bare earth.

When the day is right, about ten o'clock I put out twelve or fifteen, taking care that each hive occupies its old stand, at the same time endeavoring to take such as will be as far apart as possible; (to make this convenient, they should be carried in in the manner that you wish them to come out.)

When the rush from these hives is over, and the majority of the bees have gone back, I set out more about twelve o'clock, and when the day continues fair, another lot about two.

In the morning, while cool, I move from the back to the first apartment, about as many as I wish to set out in a day. To do this in the middle of the day, while warm, would induce a good many bees to leave the hive while the light was admitted, and would be lost.

Their long confinement makes them impatient to get out; but I have frequently returned stocks during a cold turn of weather after they had been out, and always found such equally as anxious to come out, as those which had been confined throughout the winter. Without the airings, I have kept them confined, for five months, without difficulty! The important requisites are, sufficient warmth and perfect darkness.

THE NEXT BEST PLACE FOR WINTERING BEES

A *dry*, warm cellar is the next best place for wintering them; the apiarian having one perfectly dark, with room to spare, will find it a very good place, in the absence of a room above ground. If a large number was put in, some means of ventilation should be contrived for warm turns of weather. I know an apiarian, who by my suggestion has wintered from sixty to eighty stocks in this way, for the last six years, with perfect success, not having lost one. Another has wintered thirty with equal safety.

As for burying them in the earth, I have not the least doubt, if a dry place should be selected, the hive inverted, and surrounded with hay, straw, or some substance to absorb the moisture, and protected from the rain, at the top of the covering, that perfect success would attend the experiment.

WINTERINGS IN THE OPEN AIR

As a great many beekeepers will find it inconvenient, or be unable to avail themselves of my method of wintering, it will be well enough to see how far the evils of the open air may be successfully avoided.

I am told by those who have tried wintering them in straw hives, that in this respect they are much safer than those made of boards; probably the straw will absorb the moisture. But as these hives are more trouble to construct, and their shape will prevent the use of suitable boxes for surplus honey, this one advantage will hardly balance the loss. They are said also to be more liable to injury from the moth. We want a hive that will unite advantageously as many points as possible.

It should be remembered that bees always need air, especially in the cold. With this in view, we will try to dispose of the vapor or frost. If the hive is raised sufficient to let it out, it will let in the mice. To prevent that, it should be raised only about one-fourth of an inch. The hole in the side should be nearly covered with wire cloth to keep out the mice; but give a passage for the bees; otherwise they collect here, endeavoring to get out, and remain till chilled, and thus perish by hundreds.

The boxes on the top must be removed, but not the cap or cover; the holes all opened, to let the vapor pass up into the chamber; if this is made with perfectly close joints, so that no air escapes, it should be raised a very little; otherwise not.

The moisture will condense on the sides and top, when it melts will follow the sides to the bottom, and pass out;

the rabbeting around the top of the hive will prevent its getting to the holes, and down among the bees. It will be easily comprehended, that a hole between each two combs at the top, (as mentioned in the subject of putting on the boxes,) will ventilate the hive much better than where there is but one or two, or where there is a row of several, and all are between two combs.

LITTLE RISK WITH GOOD STOCKS

All *good stocks* may be wintered in this way, with but little risk in most situations. Whether in the bleak north wind, buried in a snow-bank, or situated warm and pleasant, it will make no great difference. The mice cannot enter; the holes give them air, and carry off moisture, etc. But second-rate stocks are not equally safe in cold situations.

EFFECT OF KEEPING SECOND-RATE STOCKS OUT OF THE SUN

It has been strongly urged, without regard to the strength of the stock, to keep them all out of the sun; because an occasional warm day would call out the bees, and when they get on the snow they perish.

I have pointed out that second rate or poor stocks might occasionally starve, with plenty of stores in the hive, on account of frosty combs. If the hive is kept from the sun, in the cold, the periods of temperate weather might not occur as often, as the bees would exhaust the honey within their circle or cluster. But on the contrary, when the sun can strike the hive, it warms up the bees, and melts the frost more frequently. The bees may then go among their stores and obtain a supply as often as needed.

We seldom have a winter without sunny days enough for this purpose; but should such occur, stocks of this class should be brought into a warm room, once in four or five days, for a few hours at a time, to give them a chance to get at the honey.

Stocks much below second-rate cannot be wintered successfully in this climate; the only place for them is a warm room.

I have known bees thoroughly covered in a snowdrift, and their owner went to considerable trouble to shovel the snow away, fearing it would smother them. This is unnecessary, when protected from the mice and ventilated as just directed. A snow-bank is about as comfortable a place as they can have, except in the house.

Some recommend enclosing the whole hive by a large box set over it, making it perfectly dark, but with means for ventilation, etc. However, a snow bank would answer equally well, if not better.

EFFECTS OF SNOW CONSIDERED

As for bees getting on the snow, I apprehend that not many more are lost there than on the frozen earth.

Snow is not to be dreaded as much as chilly air. Suppose a hive stands in the sun throughout the winter, and bees are allowed to leave when they choose, and a portion are lost on the snow, and that it was possible to number all that were lost by getting chilled, throughout the season, on the bare earth – the proportion (in my opinion) lost on the snow would not be one in twenty.

Yet, I do not wish to be understood that it is of no

consequence what bees are lost on the snow. On the contrary, a great many are lost, that might be saved with proper care.

STOCKS PROTECTED ON SOME OCCASIONS

The worst time for them to leave the hive is immediately after a new snow has fallen, because if they light on it, the snow does not sustain their weight; and they soon work themselves down out of the rays of the sun, and perish.

Should it clear off pleasant, after a storm of this kind, a little attention will probably be remunerated. Also, when the weather is moderately warm, but not sufficiently so to be safe, they should be kept in, whether snow is on the ground or otherwise.

For this purpose, a wide board should be set up before the hive to protect it from the sun, at least above the entrance in the side. But if it grows sufficiently warm so that bees leave the hive when so shaded, it is a fair test by which to tell when it will do to let them sally out freely – except in cases of a new snow, when it is advisable to confine them to the hive.

The hive might be let down on the floorboard, and the wire-cloth cover the passage in the side, and made dark for the present; raising the hive at night again, as before.

I have known hundreds of stocks wintered successfully without any such care being taken, and the bees allowed to come out whenever they chose. Their subsequent health and prosperity proving that it is not altogether ruinous.

Is it not better to keep our bees warm and comfortable when practicable, as a means of saving honey?

Basics of ... Beekeeping

To winter bees in the best manner, considerable care is required. Whenever you are disposed to neglect them, you should bear in mind that one early swarm is worth two late ones; their condition in spring will often decide this point. Like a team of cattle or horses when well wintered, they are ready for a good season's work, but when poorly wintered have to recover a long time before they are worth much.

Basics of ... Beekeeping

CHAPTER TWENTY-FIVE
THE BEHAVIOR OF BEES

Writers, not content with the astonishing results of instinct, attribute a good share of reason to bees' faculties – "an adaptation of means to ends, that reason alone could produce." It is understandable one might arrive at such a conclusion for it is difficult "to tell where instinct ends and reason begins."

Instances of sagacity, like the following, have been mentioned. "When the weather is warm, and the heat inside is somewhat oppressive, a number of bees may be seen stationed around the entrance, vibrating their wings. Those inside will turn their heads towards the passage, while those outside will turn theirs the other way. A constant agitation of air is thus created, thereby ventilating the hive more effectually."

All full stocks do this in hot weather. But is it an instinctual or learned behavior?

ANOTHER EXAMPLE OF "INTELLIGENCE"

A snail had entered the hive and fixed itself against the wall. The bees, unable to penetrate its shell with their stings, fixed it immovably by cementing the shell to the wall with resin, (propolis), thus making it a prisoner for life.

How did they know the propolis they use to fill in cracks and flaws in the hive would also effectively cement the snail-shell to the wall?

Even if these things are instinctual, rather than communicated, they are nonetheless examples of group behavior.

GROUP BEHAVIOR

Eusociality is a term to describe group behavior. Generally, it involves cooperative brood care, overlapping generations, and a division of labor. The division of labor usually involves a caste system.

This group behavior is commonly observed among bees, wasps, ants, and termites.

INSTINCT vs. LEARNING

While instinct plays a major role, experiments by James Gould suggest that honeybees may have a cognitive map for information they have learned, and utilize it when communicating. For example, it's very likely they form cognitive maps of their surroundings.

Bees are known to communicate the location and nature of sources of food. And they adjust their foraging to the times at which food is available.

Foragers communicate their floral findings in order to recruit other worker bees of the hive to forage in the same area. There are two theories about how these foragers recruit other Workers — (1) Dance Theory and (2) Odor Plume Theory.

DANCE LANGUAGE

Bees are known to use a complex dance language. They use very controlled patterns of movement to deliver specific coordinates of food sources to fellow foragers.

The "waggle dance" is a figure-eight dance that shares information about the direction and distance to flowers, water sources, and potential housing locations. It consists of one to 100 circuits, each with a waggle phase and a return phase.

A "grooming dance," or "shaking dance," is performed by honeybees to initiate allogrooming – a social activity in which individuals in a group clean or maintain one another's body.

A "tremble dance" is performed by forager bees to recruit more receiver bees to help nectar.

ODOR PLUMES

Bees are very sensitive to odors (including pheromones), tastes, and colors, including ultraviolet. Keep in mind their sensitivity to smoke, a technique often used in controlling them.

Bees can be trained to perform a variety of tasks. They can learn to distinguish color through classical and operant conditioning, and they retain this information for several days.

A bee's olfactory senses rival that of a sniffer dog. They can be trained to detect explosives, drugs, and diseases.

PRIMER PHEROMONES

Pheromones are secreted or excreted chemicals that trigger a social response in members of the same species, such as bees.

TROPHALLAXIS

Information about food, temperature, thirst, and the

condition of the Queen is communicated by *Trophallaxis*, an exchange of food or fluids.

OTHER FEATS

Ethologist Karl von Frisch has demonstrated that bees can learn to count to five. And they can be trained to visit specific feeding stations at certain times of day.

PIPING

Piping is a noise made by virgin and mated Queen bees during certain times of the Queens' development. An adult Queen pipes for a two-second pulse followed by a series of quarter-second blasts. It is often described as "quacking" and "tooting."

This piping is most common when there's more than one Queen in a hive. Some theorize that piping is a "battle cry," part of the process of picking a single leader.

The surviving virgin Queen will fly out on a warm day to a "congregation area" where she will mate with a dozen or more Drones.

BUZZING

It has been hypothesized that a bee may also offer a form of communication based on the buzzing sounds made by her wings.

Basics of ... Beekeeping

CHAPTER TWENTY-SIX

STRAINING HONEY AND WAX

Honeycombs taken from the vicinity of brood-cells are generally unfit for the table, unless strained. There are several methods of doing it.

One is, to mash the comb and put it in a bag, and hang it over some vessel to catch the honey as it drains out. This will do very well for small quantities in warm weather, or in the fall before there is any of it candied.

Another method is to put such combs into a colander, and set this over a pan, and introduce it into an oven after the bread is out. This melts the combs. The honey and a portion of the wax run out together. The wax rises to the top and cools in a cake. It is somewhat liable to burn, and requires some care. Many prefer this method, as there is less taste of beebread, no cells containing it being disturbed, but all the honey is not certain to drain out without stirring it. If disposed, two qualities may be made, by keeping the first separate.

Another method is merely to break the combs finely, and put them into a colander, and allow the honey to drain out without much heat, and afterwards skim off the small particles that rise to the top, or when very particular, pass the honey through a cloth, or piece of lace.

For large quantities, a more expeditious mode is to have a can and strainer, made for the purpose, where fifty pounds or more can be worked out at once. The can is made of tin, twelve or fourteen inches deep, by about ten or twelve diameter, with handles on each side at the top, for lifting it. The strainer is just enough smaller to go down inside the can; the height may be considerably less, providing there are handles on each side to pass out at the top; the bottom is perforated with holes like a colander, combs are put into this, and the whole set into a kettle of boiling water, and heated without any risk of burning, until all the wax is melted, (which may be ascertained by stirring it,) when it may be taken out. All the wax, beebread, etc., will rise in a few minutes.

The strainer can now be raised out of the top and set on a frame for the purpose, or by merely tipping it slightly on one side it will rest on the top of the can. It might be left to cool before raising the strainer, were it not liable to stick to the sides of the can; the honey would be full as pure, and separate nearly as clean from the wax and beebread, etc.

When raised out before cooling, the contents should be repeatedly stirred, or considerable honey will remain. Two qualities may be made by keeping the first that runs through separate from the last (as stirring it works out the beebread). Even a third quality maybe obtained by adding a little water, and repeating the process. This is worth but little.

By boiling out the water, without burning, and removing the scum, it will do to feed bees. By adding water until it will just bear a potato, boiling and skimming, and letting it ferment, it will make metheglin, or by letting the fermentation proceed it will make vinegar.

Honey that has been heated thoroughly, will not candy as readily as when strained without heat. A little water may be added to prevent its getting too hard; but should it get so in cold weather, it can at any time be warmed, and water added until it is of the right consistence.

GETTING OUT WAX

Several methods have been adopted for separating the wax.

Some recommend heating it in an oven, similar to the method of straining honey through the colander, but I have found it to waste more than when melted with water. A better way for small quantities is to half fill a coarse stout bag with refuse comb and a few cobblestones to sink it, and boil it in a kettle of water, pressing and turning it frequently till the wax ceases to rise. When the contents of the bag are emptied, by squeezing a handful, the particles of wax may be seen, and you may thereby judge of the quantity thrown away.

For large quantities the foregoing process is rather tedious. It can be facilitated by having two levers four or five feet long and about four inches wide, and fastened at the lower end by a strong hinge. The combs are put into a kettle of boiling water, and will melt almost immediately; it is then put into the bag, and taken between the levers in a wash-tub or other large vessel and pressed, the contents of the bag shaken, and turned, several times during the process, and if need be returned to the boiling water and squeezed again. The wax, with a little water, is now to be remelted and strained again through finer cloth, into vessels that will mold it into the desired shape. As the sediment settles to the bottom of the wax when melted, a portion may be dipped off nearly pure without straining.

WHITENING

Wax in cool weather may be whitened in a short time in the sun, but it must be in very thin flakes; it is readily obtained in this shape by having a very thin board or shingle, which should be first thoroughly wet, and then dipped into pure melted wax; enough will adhere to make it the desired thickness, and will cool instantly on being withdrawn. Draw a knife along the edges, and it will readily cleave off. Exposed to the sun in a window or on the snow, it will become perfectly white, when it can be made into cakes for market, where it commands a much higher price than the yellow.

Basics of ... Beekeeping

CHAPTER TWENTY-EIGHT

COLONY COLLAPSE DISORDER AND GMOs

Bees are disappearing. The term Colony Collapse Disorder (CCD) describes a phenomenon in which worker bees are disappearing, causing entire bee colonies to collapse.

EINSTEIN'S WARNING
A quote attributed to Albert Einstein states:

If the bee disappeared off the surface of the globe then man would only have four years of life left. No more bees, no more pollination, no more plants, no more animals, no more man.

A dire prediction, even if there's no evidence that Einstein ever said it.

HISTORY OF COLONY COLLAPSE DISORDER
This concern is not new. After all, such disappearances have occurred throughout the history of apiculture. These has been known by various names including *Disappearing Disease, Spring Dwindle, May Disease, Autumn Collapse,* and *Fall Dwindle Disease*. The syndrome was renamed *Colony Collapse Disorder* in late 2006.

The causes behind Colony Collapse Disorder are

unclear. Some theories blame pesticides, primarily neonicoptinoids; various pathogens; infections with Varroa and Acarapis mites; malnutrition; genetic factors; immunodeficiencies; loss of suitable habitat; changing beekeeping practices; electronic signals; or a combination thereof.

A $200 BILLION THREAT

Colony collapse is economically significant because agricultural crops worldwide are pollinated by honeybees. According to the Agriculture and Consumer Protection Department of the Food and Agriculture Organization of the United Nations, global crops depending on honeybee's pollination was estimated to be worth close to $200 billion.

THOUSANDS OF VARIETIES OF PLANTS

In 1901 Nobel prizewinner Maurice Maeterlinck published this pronouncement in "The Life of the Bee":

"You will probably more than once have seen her fluttering about the bushes, in a deserted corner of your garden, without realizing that you were carelessly watching the venerable ancestor to whom we probably owe most of our flowers and fruits (for it is actually estimated that more than a hundred thousand varieties of plants would disappear if the bees did not visit them), and possibly even our civilization, for in these mysteries all things intertwine."

GENETICALLY MODIFIED ORGANISM

A Genetically Modified Organism (GMO) is an

organism whose genetic material has been altered using genetic engineering techniques. Organisms that have been genetically modified include microorganisms such as bacteria and yeast, as well as insects, plants, fish, and mammals.

GMOs are the source of genetically modified foods. Commercial sale of genetically modified crops began in 1994, with the introduction of the Flavr Savr delayed ripening tomato.

Much controversy exists over GM foods. In particular, there are movements to require specific labeling.

GM BEES

Genetically Modified Organisms (GMO's) are a highly contentious topic these days, and blamed by some for the demise of bees.

GE crops have been widely adopted in U.S. agriculture, and thus are now a part of beekeeping.

While Monsanto researchers insist there is no strong evidence that the spraying of generic glyphosate herbicide is directly causing significant bee mortality, Drs. Jim and Maryann Frazier raise legitimate concerns about the effect of some adjuvants—especially the organ silicones.

This herbicidal elimination of flowering weeds severely reduces the plants available for bee forage.

The scientific farming of corn, soybeans, sunflowers, or squashes has eliminated many weeds that provided alternative nectar and pollen sources for bees. Today, there is often nary a bee-nutritious weed to be seen in or around a field of corn or soybeans.

Basics of ... Beekeeping

BEE PRODUCTS

Materials scientist Debbie Chachra has been researching "bee plastic," a cellophane-like biopolymer produced by *Colletes inaequalis*, a species of bee native to New England.

"The bees are pretty much just eating pollen and producing this plastic, and we're trying to understand how they do it," says Chachra. "More intriguingly, the cellophane-like bee plastic doesn't come from petroleum."

New York-based designer John Becker has proposed using genetically modified bees to produce concrete instead of honey, turning them into miniature repair services for crumbling urban structures.

A Brave New World, indeed.

Basics of ... Beekeeping

CHAPTER TWENTY-NINE

PURCHASING STOCKS AND TRANSPORTING BEES

If the reader owns no bees, yet has had enough interest to follow this *Basics of* ... guide to its end, that is evidence you possess the requisite perseverance to become a beekeeper.

It would be well, however, to remind you of the anxieties, perplexities, and time involved in taking proper care of bees. But if you remain disposed to try beekeeping, some further directions are required to get you started.

WHY THE WORD LUCK IS APPLIED TO BEES

Some apiarists have been successful, while others have failed entirely. This has suggested that *luck* depends on the manner that the stocks were obtained.

You have lots of options:

Some will assert that the "fickle dame" is charmed into favor by stealing a stock or two to begin with, and returning them after a start. Another, (a little more conscientious, perhaps) that you must take them without *liberty*, to be sure, but leave an equivalent in money on the stand. And still another says that *bees must always be a gift*.

I suggest you buy them.

There are many sources for purchasing bees. You can even buy them on Amazon. A single caged Queen honeybee goes for $29.95, while you can get a 3-pound

Basics of ... Beekeeping

package of bees along with a caged Queen for $154.95 plus shipping. A 10-frame hive costs $157.99 and stainless steel smokers are priced at $20.50 each. You might want to consider the beehive starter kit for $

The description reads:

"Get all you need to start beekeeping in one package! This is the perfect Bee Hive Starter Kit for beginners as well as pros. Please note: the Deep Hive Body and the Medium Hive Super will come to you assembled & painted. This is a great opportunity to help your local environment and to start having years of fun! Items Included: 1 Telescoping Lid, 1 Inner Cover, 1 Finger Joint Medium Super, 10 Medium Frames Assembled with Crimped Wired Foundation, 1 Finger Joint Deep Hive Body, 10 Deep Frames Assembled with Crimped Wired Foundation, 1 Screened Bottom Board, 1 Screened Bottom Board Mite Tray, 1 Entrance Reducer, 1 Entrance Feeder, 1 Hive Tool, 1 Smoker, 1 Bee Brush, 1 Pair of Goatskin Gloves (please specify size), 1 Bee Jacket (please specify size), 1 Book: First Lessons in Bee Keeping."

I would recommend purchasing none but first-rate stocks.

It will make little difference whether you obtain them in the spring or fall, if you have read the foregoing remarks on management with attention.

If your bees prosper, the money that stocks cost is a mere trifle in comparison to the increase in value that you'll see.

GIFT OR SHARES

Should anyone feel disposed to make you a present of

a stock or two of bees, I would advise you to accept the offer and be thankful. Or if anyone is willing you should take some bees on shares, this is a cheap way to get a start, and you have no risk of loss.

RULE IN TAKING BEES FOR A SHARE

The rule generally adopted for taking bees is this. One or more stocks are taken for a term of years, the person taking them finding hives, boxes, and bestowing whatsoever care is necessary, and returning the old stocks to the owner with half the increase and profits.

MODERATE WEATHER BEST TO REMOVE BEES

In transporting your bees, avoid the two extremes of very cold or very warm weather.

In the warm weather, the combs are so nearly melted that the weight of the honey will bend them, bursting the cells, spilling the honey, and besmearing the bees.

In very cold weather, the combs are brittle and easily detached from the sides of the hive. When necessitated to move them in very cold weather, they should be put up an hour or so before starting. The agitation of the bees after being disturbed will create considerable heat; a portion of this will be imparted to the combs, and add to their strength.

PREPARATIONS FOR TRANSPORTING BEES

To prepare for moving the hive, pieces of thin muslin about half a yard square is as good as anything, secured by carpet tacks.

SECURING BEES IN THE HIVE

The hive is inverted, and the cloth put over, and fastened with a tack at the corners and another in the middle. The tack is crowed in about two-thirds of its length, so tat it presents a head convenient to pull out. If the bees are to go a great distance, and require to be shut up several days, the muslin will be hardly sufficient, as they would probably bite their way out. Something more substantial would then be required.

Take a board the size of the bottom, cut out a place in the middle, and cover with wire cloth, (like the one recommended for hiving,) and fasten it with tacks. This board is to be nailed on the hive. After the nails are driven, with the hammer start it off about the eighth of an inch; it will admit a little air around the sides as well as the middle, quite necessary for heavy stocks.

But very small families might be safe without the wire cloth; air enough would pass between the hive and board, except in warm weather. New combs break easier than old.

BEST CONVEYANCE

Probably the best conveyance is a pickup truck with elliptic springs. Any vehicle without good springs is not recommended, especially for transporting young stocks. Yet I have known them moved safely in this way, but it required some care in packing with hay, or straw, under and around them, and careful driving.

HIVE TO BE INVERTED

Whatever conveyance is employed, the hive should be inverted. The combs will then all rest closely on the top, and are less liable to break than when right end up, because then the whole weight of the combs must depend upon the fastenings at the top and sides for support, and are easily detached and fall.

When moving bees, so reversed, they will creep upward. In stocks part full, they will often leave the combs and get upon the covering. In a short time after being set up, they will return, except in very cold weather, when a few will sometimes freeze; consequently a warm room is required to put them in for a short time.

After carrying them a few miles, the disposition to sting is generally gone, yet there are a few exceptions. In moderate weather, when bees are confined, they manifest a persevering determination to find their way out, particularly after being moved, and somewhat disturbed. I have known them to bite holes through muslin in three days.

The same difficulty is often attendant on attempting to confine them to the hive by muslin when in the house in the winter, except when kept in a cold situation. Should any combs become broken, or detached from their fastenings, in hives not full, by moving or other accident, rendering them liable to fall when set up, the hive may remain inverted on the stand till warm weather, if necessary, and the bees have again fastened them, which they do soon after commencing work in the spring. If they are so badly broken that they bend over, rolls of paper may be put between them to preserve the proper distance till secured.

When they commence making new combs, or before, it is time to turn the right end up. While the hive is inverted, it is essential that a hole is in the side, through which the bees may work. A board should fit close over the bottom, and covered, to effectually prevent any water from getting among the bees, etc.

CONCLUSION

In conclusion I would say, the apiarian who has followed this guide attentively has acquired a great amount of knowledge about bees.

It has been said that "three out of five who commence an apiary must fail." But I would say to the beginner – *See your bees often, and at all times be aware of their actual condition*. This one recipe is worth more than all others that can be given.

With the above motto acted upon, carried out fully, and you will realize success.

The careless, inattentive apiarists who leaves his bees unnoticed from October till May, will likely meet with failure.

That said, I would encourage all who are interested to try their skill in bee management. Is there, in the whole of nature, any science more inviting than this? Apiculture – what more exalting activity, while at the same time offering a pecuniary reward?

Lorenzo Lorraine Langstroth

Thank you for reading.
Please review this book. Reviews help others find Absolutely Amazing eBooks and inspire us to keep providing these marvelous tales.

If you would like to be put on our email list to receive updates on new releases, contests, and promotions, please go to AbsolutelyAmazingEbooks.com and sign up.

AbsolutelyAmazingEbooks.com
or AA-eBooks.com

www.ingramcontent.com/pod-product-compliance
Lightning Source LLC
Chambersburg PA
CBHW070734160426
43192CB00009B/1433